MW00834813

FROM THEOLOGY TO THEOLOGICAL THINKING

Richard Lectures for 2010

From Theology to Theological Thinking

JEAN-YVES LACOSTE

TRANSLATED BY W. CHRIS HACKETT

WITH AN INTRODUCTION
BY JEFFREY BLOECHL

UNIVERSITY OF VIRGINIA PRESS
CHARLOTTESVILLE AND LONDON

University of Virginia Press
© 2014 by the Rector and Visitors of the University of Virginia
All rights reserved
Printed in the United States of America on acid-free paper

First published 2014

ISBN 978-0-8139-3556-0

9 8 7 6 5 4 3 2 1

Library of Congress Cataloging-in-Publication Data is available
from the Library of Congress.

Contents

Eschatology, Liturgy, and the Task of Thinking

JEFFREY BLOECHL

Our question today, and perhaps always, asks not whether God exists but what God's relation is to the world. This question troubles the life of faith, and it challenges the theology that provides that life with its necessary intelligence. And one misses its full force if one reduces it to a matter of divine mystery, where to be sure thought does meet an essential limit. The difficulty of knowing God's relation to the world is also rooted in the difficulty of the world itself, with its multiple and shifting opacities and the charm that they exercise on our native and naive desire. We may rightly expect an improved understanding of the life of faith from a deeper understanding of the world, of the desire that sometimes aims beyond it to God but that also and—how to deny it?—far more often continues to circulate within the world and everything in it. For a Christian, Divine transcendence is preserved behind the Word spoken once and for all in this world, so that interpreting that Word is a worldly enterprise whose fulfillment must be precisely eschatological. But the immanence of this world is not therefore laid bare for us to see according to a different sort of illumination that would be once and for all. As milieu, as horizon for concerns that are in the first instance strictly material, the world eludes us not because it is, as is God above all, too distant, too much and too far beyond our reach, but instead because it is too near to us, so that every reach already presumes it and passes over it, if only to often sink back toward it. The life of faith moves perpetually between that distance and that nearness, and the thinking that attends to such a life must reckon with both of them.

In our account of "world," it is necessary to resist a temptation to move immediately to what cosmology and metaphysics appear to have meant, that is, to move to some conception of a domain that exhibits coordinates that are independent of any human relation to them. Already before this thought arises, "world" is first our relation to spatiality and indeed the temporality that, as Bergson has shown, is all too often thought in terms that are fundamentally spatial. This existential conception of world has been explored best and most recently by phenomenology, which thus presents itself as a new *ancilla theologiae*. Such has been an important point of departure for Jean-Yves Lacoste, whose work specifies further that when it is a matter of phenomenology then it is above all Heidegger that we must heed. There are texts in which Lacoste refers to Heidegger as "the Philosopher," consciously echoing Aquinas's name for Aristotle. The gesture has a general significance and one that is quite particular. On the one hand, Lacoste's predilection for Heidegger is defended along the same line as that of the Angelic Doctor for his pagan teacher: the works of the Philosopher offer us the best possible understanding of dimensions of our being that do not (yet) know God; and while the believing thinker is inclined to consider these dimensions as somehow incomplete or dark, insofar as they clearly are intelligible and exhibit a viable integrity all their own, they must be considered as genuine possibilities internal to the complete way of life that is illumined by an openness to God. On the other hand, this is specifically a matter of what modern thought has begun to call our "secularity," though of course the notion of the *secular* is as old as that of a distinction between Creator and creatures who are given a truly distinct existence. Here the phenomenological approach unquestionably provides us with a new clarification: our secularity, our this-worldiness, is existential—or, if we may risk this word so close to the philosophy of Heidegger, anthropological—before it is natural, cosmological, or broadly metaphysical. And of course, readers of *Sein und Zeit* think immediately of Heidegger's conception of *in-der-Welt-Sein*, which now appears as both the fundamental condition for a way of life that remains entirely deaf to the Word and a primordial dimension of a somewhat different way of life that hears the Word and yet also knows itself to be bound to objects, tools, food, and indeed the milieu in which they present themselves. Is this conception of our secularity, including the ambivalence we have just assigned to it, anywhere to be found in the work of Thomas Aquinas? If not, and unless it is more than the name of a confusion, we may follow Lacoste's implication, in many works, that in our own time we are confronted with a new, ongoing clarification of quite what it means to be not only toward-God but also, and at the same time, irrevocably, in-the-world. There is an entire theology of history contained in this deployment of an essentially phenomenological notion.

—⊗—

Between 1990 and 1998 Jean-Yves Lacoste published two important books supported by numerous articles, and the landmark *Dictionnaire critique de théologie*.[1] Both of the books are dominated in their approaches and in the constitution of their problematics by an encounter with Heidegger. The first of them, *Note sur le temps* (1990, as yet untranslated into English), proposes to explore the temporal dimension of a comprehensive logic of our being. After a preliminary philosophical hermeneutic, Lacoste introduces a theological conception unfolded from the Incarnation, understood as the entrance of the Absolute in time. In a third step, he sketches the theological constitution of historicity, that is to say, of the lived time from which the sequences of events and constellations of relations belonging to history are born and receive their proper meaning. The philosophical hermeneutic underlines that it is Husserl who has best reminded us that our relations with the world and everything in it are irreducibly corporeal, but contends that if we wish to follow this notion through to its essential implication for temporality we must turn finally to Heidegger. Where else may we define the time of the body if not in a relation to our mortality? Our body is our insertion in the world (Merleau-Ponty), and its temporality is defined by a relation to an end that weighs upon us as a future to be met. And this meeting occurs, uniquely or not, in what Heidegger understands as anxiety at one's own death. Husserl's phenomenology of the body has overlooked this, and in that respect failed to bring corporeality and temporality together in the manner that Heidegger has done, notwithstanding the well-known paucity of his references to the body. This leads Heideggerian thought to affirm that "death would in fact be the eschatology of meaning."[2] If it may seem that all of phenomenology until and including Merleau-Ponty has either accepted this notion or rejected eschatology altogether, it is clear that the emergence of subsequent, self-styled counter-phenomenologies currently in vogue are defined to a considerable degree by their wish to overcome it. It is instructive to see that Lacoste's particular manner of resistance has set him somewhat apart from all of these approaches already from this earliest book.

For Lacoste, meaning is not determined solely by our relation to our death, because mortality is not the sole defining figure of our finitude. In a certain sense, his phenomenological work has long been concerned with establishing precisely this. The effort is in fact strikingly modest. The account of our finitude proposed especially in *Sein und Zeit* is neither rejected nor submitted to a more primordial horizon so much as interrupted by a series of examples and a defense of their irreducibility to the precepts of fundamental ontology. Moreover, this is undertaken without ever denying that those examples will not submit to the principles of orthodox phenomenology:[3] ethical life demands a relation with infinity that can no more be made to appear than be rejected out of hand because it does not appear, the sacraments are inscribed in history without submitting to claims that they be understood as the expression of a meaning that is finally and only historical, and between the Incarnation and the Resurrection unfold the reasons for a hope that cannot be realized in this world and yet does find a distinctive way of being there. This last claim is evidently of supreme importance. In *Note sur le temps*, the hope of the believer is carefully distinguished from any form of expectation or anticipation that would take aim at a realizable fulfillment. Hope in the promise of Resurrection is hope for a beatitude that comes, if it comes, in its own time, which is to say not the time of care, morality, and the being in the world that Heidegger has examined.

This is a fertile idea, if also a familiar one. Henri de Lubac has reminded us, several decades ago, that the *eschaton* is beyond any one person's reach first of all because it defines the future not solely of the individual but of the entire community of believers (Lacoste makes note of it, in an article contributed to his *Dictionnaire*).[4] This manner of embedding community and thus plurality in eschatology is also present in *Note sur le temps*, where it interrupts and contests the Heideggerian hermeneutics of being in the world as care (*Sorge*). Of course, broadly speaking this has also been the attempt made by Levinas, though there is never any doubt in any of Lacoste's work that a personal, religious relation with the Absolute God must be distinguished from, and even put in reciprocal critique with, the ethical relation among human beings.[5] Interestingly, Lacoste does agree with Levinas that the ethical relation, no less than the religious (or as he will later call it, the "liturgical"), relation with God exceeds the logic that prevails over our existence in the world. But his way of conceiving ethics and religion does not require us to reject the philosophy of Heidegger so much as to accept it under the proviso that it not be permitted to occlude our view of a dimension of humanity that fundamental ontology and its hermeneutics of Dasein has not been able to recognize. In short, and as I began by suggesting, the latter may contribute important new insight into our being in the world, understood as our this-worldliness, which is to say our secularity. It would probably be going too far to propose that Heidegger offers us a philosophical account of Christian fallenness (a notion to which he himself, at any rate, was strongly opposed), yet we might consider him to have helped us to better understand the possibility of everything that we are accustomed to associate with fallenness—fallibility, fault, and so forth—all of which undoubtedly do find a root in our mortality. If this is Lacoste's approach to Heidegger, then unlike Levinas or for that matter Marion, he thinks it possible and perhaps even necessary to incorporate the findings of a text like *Sein und Zeit* positively into a project that is, if not robustly theological, at least actively sympathetic to theological phenomena.

This is enough for us to look with new interest at the possibility that philosophy itself operates within a horizon that is properly eschatological. Of course, if we follow Lacoste this far, the eschatology in question cannot be ordered either to death (Heidegger) or to ultimate conditions that may be realized in human history (Hegel, Marx). We find an analysis of such immanent eschatologies in terms of the conceptions of reason on which they depend in some late work by Jean Ladrière.[6] It belongs to human being that it may aim to grasp itself and speak of itself to itself in discourse. This self-grasp and self-disclosure can be pursued only in and through a realization of oneself as immersed in the world, itself understood as a universal condition. According to Ladrière, philosophy develops from this insight and attempts to form and then address an order of knowledge (*epistēmēe*). Insofar as this order is projected ahead of an exploration of the world that would confirm or adjust its definition, it is necessarily an ideal. Philosophy thus constitutes reason, by which that exploration would take place, in view of an ideal. In turn, this raises the thought that under strict philosophical guidance reason might attain, in and through an adequate grasp of its authentic condition, complete intelligibility—and inversely, that this intelligibility would appear as the essential content of reflective reason. Evidently enough, philosophies aligned with logic and mathematics might well pursue this vision as if truly within our reach. But those that recognize the historicity and indeed the facticity of meaning instead frame their approach to an *eschaton* of reason in an acceptance, and therefore an interpretation, of essential limits. Yet it is enough to suppose that the movement of reason is at heart a movement of self-constitution that strives to understand everything else in its own light for it to become clear that the very possibility of reason is ensured by the thought of some ultimate fulfillment. The moment philosophy admits the historicity and facticity of meaning, it becomes inevitable that this fulfillment will be conceived in terms of an event by which what was previously out of reach, perhaps hidden, at last comes to light. Should this truly come to pass in our own time, under our own powers, the *eschaton* of reason would appear in the recapitulation of every particular phase or fragment but now as a provisional figure of the universal. Refusing such a totalization by insisting on the inaccessibility of the *eschaton* to the reason that thinks it, Lacoste commits philosophy to a principle that does elevate it but at the same time humbles it, and that stimulates it without owing it anything. And to be sure, this does not abandon philosophy to nihilism, but on the contrary holds nihilism at bay precisely by insisting on the preeminence of a word that is both final because it has not yet been properly heard and first because it has already been spoken. The "theological thinking" that is a preoccupation of Lacoste's 2010 Richard Lectures may be taken to emanate from this achievement.

Lacoste's second book, *Expérience et Absolu* (translated as *Experience and the Absolute*), extends the work begun in his first one along at least two important lines. On the one hand, Lacoste rejects the modern habit of grounding religious thought in the category of experience (e.g., Schleiermacher) and in its place proposes an account of our "liturgical" relation with God. On the other hand, he also rejects any attempt to submit the meaning of that relation to the self-authenticating reason of a system (e.g., Hegel). These two efforts are of a single piece. To exist *coram Deo* is not to feel the constant presence of the divine but on the contrary to sometimes, perhaps often, suffer precisely the failure or lack of such a presence—and of course as the failure or lack of what one genuinely wants most. There is no single reason for this, unless it is simply our mortality (and to the degree that this is the case, Heidegger must remain close to the analysis): the world and the earth claim us no less constantly than God, our consciences are mixed and unsettled, and at any rate God is [↗] not compelled by either human desire or human time. Some of Lacoste's most challenging passages struggle to develop our relation with God in full view of these difficulties. In their course one finds an entire field of new concepts worthy of separate attention: inexistence, non-experience, non-event, non-place, and (although here the inspiration is avowedly Sanjuanist) vigil and night. Let us note their most forceful implication: it may be that the contemporary experience of Godlessness is not only, but terribly, the expression of some great fall in Western culture but also, at the same time, the gigantic expression of a possibility already contained within the very nature of our relation with the Absolute God. We may leave it for others to decide whether this underlines a religious legitimacy for much of what is most troubling in the contemporary ethos. In the meantime, one cannot help being provoked by the image of a close passage between those whose being in the world may take the form of longing for a God who does not always come, and those whose being in the world no longer includes a meaningful relation to that longing.

For reasons that may already be evident, one finds in *Expérience et Absolu* a striking convergence of phenomenological interpretation and dialectical critique. Where it is a matter of liturgy, of a living relation with the Absolute God, every dynamic belonging properly to our existence, as inherence in the world, is checked and put out of play. Or conversely, it is precisely when experience fails—when it is necessary to invoke the possibility of non-experience—that we must contemplate a dimension of our humanity not framed exclusively in the horizon of our relation with the world and everything in it. But these claims are also part of a comprehensive theory of our "humanity."[7] As we have noted, Lacoste's thinking goes quite far toward recognizing as

INTRODUCTION

distinctive and viable the way of life that knows only our relation with the world, in its most expansive sense, as the ground and source of meaning. It is doubtful, then, that he would fully accept the expression sometimes favored by de Lubac (to whom *Expérience et Absolu* is dedicated), for whom this way of life must receive the negative designation "unbelief." For when, initially following de Lubac, Lacoste takes reflection to sufficient height from which to consider belief and nonbelief alongside one another, what he sees in the latter is not a distorted or defunct desire for God but only a desire that is as naturally inclined to the world that captivates it as to the God who is the principle of that world. This is confirmed at the heart of *Expérience et Absolu*, in a hypothesis on which a considerable portion of Lacoste's originality in fact seems to depend: faced with the phenomenon of nonbelief, it is not necessary to choose between the perverse choices of a fallen human will and the mystery of a transcendent divine will; there is also a "muteness" already in being, by which even the most sincere desire may lose its way. In the text, this is said in response above all to Rahner, whose notions of a religious apriori and a "transcendental experience" of God seem bound to arrive at such a severe alternative (and its well-known impasses).[8] But it might also be directed, more generally, to the strangely modern preoccupation with a false opposition between nature and supernature, and indeed at more than one point Lacoste does address that problem.[9]

In *Expérience et Absolu* these and related matters are brought together in an attempt to grasp what is proper to the religious dimension of our humanity, but without pretending that that dimension could ever be fully uncoupled from a secular dimension. If, according to a habit of Lacoste's own texts, we understand this with the help of terms borrowed from Heideggerian phenomenology, we might ascribe to our humanity both a susceptibility to captivation by the world and the earth, and the awakening of something like a foretaste of the Absolute God. And we might recognize signs of their distinct presences in us in certain moods that befall us as we submit to one or the other of them. The early Heidegger has already found one such sign in the mood of anxiety, in which he sees an attunement to being (as nothingness). The later Heidegger considers the mood of serenity to signal an attunement to what he calls "earth." Lacoste accepts both of these, but gestures toward the existence of yet another: religious joy, as the mood in which we may glimpse the blossoming of an attunement properly to God.[10]

Now as Heidegger also showed, a mood and an attunement are always accompanied by a distinct mode of understanding, so that those two together might in principle unfold an entire worldview (*Sein und Zeit* §§31–32). Heidegger's constant reference is Dasein, as being in the world. Lacoste's proposal is that being toward God is not wholly separable from being in the world, which is to say that those who find themselves attuned to God and understanding the world according to a relation with God must contend with an attunement and an understanding that are otherwise defined. If we do not always recognize this tension in ourselves, then we may be in need of a luminous example to bring it to light. For this reason, and undoubtedly others, Lacoste, like Stanislas Breton before him,[11] welcomes the spectacle of the Holy Fools, in whose subversion of worldly wisdom we may glimpse possibilities—and finally their source: a *soul*—uncontained by the world in which the Fools, and less dramatically we, nonetheless "inhere."[12]

At such a point, the critical function of phenomenology for Lacoste's work brings us to the threshold of the theology that it may serve. There is nothing especially new in the thought that the world and the earth exercise a charm that may hinder the desire that seeks the God who is the principle of their being. Theology has always recognized and intervened in this drama, presenting itself as the light by which to witness its true meaning. Yet neither this conception of our condition nor that classical role for theology has retained its original force into the most recent centuries. We are moderns insofar as we accede to a rationality that appears to affirm the primacy of this world, its presence, and the meaning of things that do not owe their intelligibility to anything beyond that horizon. To the considerable degree that such a modernity has claimed priority in our thinking, the texts by which Lacoste contests it are more than a renewal of certain theological impulses. They are also, when addressing themselves to present circumstances, the most untimely of meditations.

A good number of the foregoing themes are profiled in the remarkable *Dictionnaire critique de théologie*. Virtually all of the expected theological topics receive careful study. Moreover, the entries (of which there are well over 500) generally balance historical accounts with systematic reflection, most often in distinct parts. One is provided with a review of developments from the appearance of a principle or practice already in scripture, and then the manner in which the tradition has understood them from the patristic period into the twentieth century. But one also finds helpful guidance in developing a critical interpretation of the concepts and questions that are generated along the way. Indeed, precisely this is advertised by the title of the *Dictionnaire*, which sets out to work "critically" rather than dogmatically. Accordingly, one should not be overly surprised to find a considerable amount of attention reserved for modernity, modern theology, and distinctly modern problems.[13] Nor, given what we have seen thus far, should one be surprised to find that the heart of Lacoste's position on modernity, perhaps even in the *Dictionnaire*, appears most distinctly in his own entry on Heidegger. The final lines of the entry say a great deal: "theology has nothing to learn [from its encounter with Heidegger] except that it is not everything, though this is a very useful lesson."[14] We have already seen enough of Lacoste's thinking for it to be clear that this a remark of great depth. It is nonetheless worth adding that this does seem to undercut an entire way of theologizing that takes its bearings from the lived experience and historical-cultural context in which the meaning of faith is generated. Not that Lacoste, with his serious appreciation of Heidegger, would ever for a moment resist claims for the historicity of meaning. But the remark does make heard—and here it simply echoes major claims stated in his own books—a proposal that in the final account we submit the historicity of meaning to the auto-donation of God.

We will leave for another occasion any attempt to pursue the theological debate opened here. It will have to suffice for us to note, first, that it has also been opened by, among others, Jean Greisch, when addressing himself to the same line of the same entry on Heidegger.[15] To this we may add, second, that for his part Lacoste has in his subsequent books preferred to apply himself to the problematic of phenomenality as such, especially seeking an account of that field which will admit what we have just called the "auto-donation of God" without thereby diminishing our sensitivity to other modes of givenness.[16] And then finally, let us venture to say of Lacoste's most recent book, *Être et danger,* that it proposes something approaching a summary statement of what has been undertaken since *Expérience et Absolu:* between phenomenology and theology, it is not necessary to decide, and for at least two reasons.[17] On the one hand, and as Lacoste's earlier work has contended, it is possible to expand the range of phenomenological research to achieve, if not simple comprehension of the things of faith, then at least an admission of their independent possibility—and moreover, a possibility that does appear. On the other hand, and as Lacoste's most recent work has begun to contend, both modes of reflection must contend with an entire range of phenomena situated along the border between appearing and nonappearing, each of which, at least as a type, exhibits a mode of givenness that possesses its own affective tonality, which is to say, in *grosso modo,* its own mode of reaching consciousness. Needless to say, this work constitutes a further elaboration of the phenomenology that Lacoste would hold open to phenomena previously considered inadmissible there. It probably also goes without saying that this is hardly alien to the theological question we uncovered in commenting on his *Dictionnaire.*

—⁂—

The three texts assembled in the present volume develop their proposals by way of masterful work in the history of theology and philosophy. But their argument is neither strictly historical nor, depending on the operative definitions, strictly philosophical or theological (and even calls such disciplinary regimes into question). Most of its defining features have already been developed in Lacoste's previous texts. If the liturgical relation is admitted into an expanded phenomenology by the discovery of an enriched sense of affectivity—if, in other words, our relation with the Absolute God is anchored in pre-predicative experiences that animate an entire way of life that nonetheless also admits a wide range of other relations and experiences, *each in its own right*—then it is the primary task of any theology that takes cognizance of this discovery to provide concepts that are adequate to the full richness of what we may venture to call "liturgical man." It is crucial to these lectures that for Lacoste the thinking that this requires would by definition have to avoid every manner of system or school, suspecting in them a return of the onto-theological metaphysics that Heidegger has been right to define and criticize, whether or not he has always been right in identifying it with particular authors or texts. We have already touched on an important goal of this avoidance: thinking would thus attempt not only to free religious meaning from the bounds of immanence but also to ward off the charge of nihilism first voiced by Nietzsche. More immediately, it would also affirm the finite human context in which concepts are proposed according to an art of living amid phenomena that present themselves first as possibilities, which is to say—and in themselves not at all—according to the necessity that is enforced by a logic of ulterior commitments.

From the beginning of these lectures, Lacoste has grasped this living root of true thinking, and throughout them he reminds us of the difficulties that face any attempt to keep it in view. The very fact that one's thinking is animated by—if we may recur to an earlier notion—a specific attunement goes hand in hand with the notion that the thinking in question is exposed to the vagaries that belong to affectivity. This enables one to see that the great schools and disciplines that are promoted within philosophy and theology were defined first in order to preserve not only a way of life but also the way of thinking that becomes possible there. Theory does not propose limits for how to live except according to a sense of life in which it is felt that adherence to those limits leads us toward the fulfillment of some important promise. It is no doubt true that this much remains close to things we have learned from Pierre Hadot, for example, and part of the lesson does consist in seeing, as Hadot also makes us see, the boundary between philosophy and theology all but disappear. That said, it is difficult to miss Lacoste's proposal that it may be to the theological tradition that we should turn first in order to recover a language for this sensibility that a proclivity for institutions, disciplines, and professions—on the part of theologians no less than philosophers—has sometimes threatened to make us forget. What I take to be the crucial references in his lectures return us inevitably to the notion of spirituality—not as a "soft" or clouded form of speculation, but on the contrary as the pure form of the very possibility of speculation. Here we might think first of John of the Cross, though Lacoste offers us many other examples. The poems, let us remember, are almost immediate expressions of a profound experience and a new, well-defined outlook. The later, technical work of the *Ascent* is already two steps removed from experiences that nonetheless stand in need of the concepts that it supplies.[18]

Nothing prevents us from associating these notions with what we have already encountered in the form of a thinking that is properly eschatological. Nor is there anything in the way of associating them with the correction of Heideggerian topologies of world and earth enacted by the range of analyses that refuse its limits in favor of the liturgical relation. Neither time nor space is enclosed by a logic capable of anticipating every possibility, and the thinking that is truly deserving of the name takes hold in sensitivity to the double expression of our finitude that this entails. Heidegger's later work includes a call to fashion our thinking closer to such a sensitivity. It is not certain that this can succeed without admitting the possibility of an Absolute God. If this is so, then it may well be that it is theology, and not philosophy, that may offer us the way to a form of reflection that truly attends to the condition of our humanity. It is this that Lacoste proposes to call *theological thinking*.

A Note on the Translation

W. CHRIS HACKETT

It is perhaps a paradox that translators, at least the honest ones, attempt to hide themselves through their work. John Scotus Erigena, the Irish thinker, is a famous example. As the translator of the Dionysian corpus into Latin in the tenth century, he "introduced" apophatic theology into the Latin context. He also transformed it (in this way he only pushed in a new direction Pseudo-Dionysius's own unique, Christian transformation of the religious impulse within Neoplatonism). This inevitable transformation was therefore not merely the result of the transfer through Erigena's pen of something born in one world of thought, the Greek one, into another, alien world, the Latin one. Erigena also self-consciously and perhaps duplicitously (since he explicitly denied it in his preface to the *Areopagitica;* see *Patrologia Latina* 122, 1032 B–C) developed what he received, which marked a clear transformation that will only come to reach its most concrete historical form in Thomas Aquinas. Erigena translated the Dionysian corpus for reasons having to do with his own theological-philosophical questions. It is truly fitting in this and every case that "translator" is, in Latin, *interpres.* Nevertheless, this hiding or masking or self-erasure normatively has as its end in the first place pure transparency or duplication. And however distinct the mediums of this duplication, French and English, they are nevertheless both included in the same set of things called "language." (The measure of the success of this

task is thankfully not determined by the relation of "duplication" to "duplicity," Erigena notwithstanding.) Such "transparency" is no doubt—as we "critical thinkers" today know only
all too well—an "infinite task" in its own right, always receding
beyond the horizon of the work that is produced. Repetition
is non-identical, particularly when the repetition is a translation. The translator is himself the passage from one language
to another, one world of thought to another, and his thinking,
his reception and understanding of the text, is ever-present in
the work that he renders. The path of transition is also always
one of transformation. Every word and phrase carries with it
the necessity of a choice among a multitude of possible render-
ings; philosophical concepts in particular are among the most
pernicious choices to make, and never quite meet up, in their
own irreducible complexity, with that of the word they stand in
for. (The reader will thank me for sparing him any neologism in
the text—I did use the word "scientificity" for *scientificité*, which
means something like "characterized by a correspondence to the
criteria of science." It is perhaps self-evident why I employed it,
and it is not exactly a neologism: Terry Eagleton used it in 1976
in *Criticism and Ideology*.) Try as he might, the translator therefore leaves his mark on the text he translates. The translator's
work is not description, but transposition and interpretation.
He must think in order to do his work. So in however a minor
way my thinking, unfortunate for you, marks this text from end
to end. And such, anyway, is the micro-drama (and excitement)
of translation. Now this marking is for the most part, I hope,
invisible: fidelity to the original text and even to the "mind" and
"spirit" of the author were my goals. No Erigenian "faithful
duplicity" here.

Translation is, as you can no doubt surmise, an arduous and
painstaking labor. It is fraught with difficulties, blind lanes, dead
ends—and inevitably, mistakes. It brings with it little glory in
the present academic "regime," which, in its quantitative (and,
let me soberly add, nihilist) metrics of "learning outcomes" does
not recognize translation's importance for "the advancement of

knowledge" not to mention its place as a serious contribution to a field of research. The pay is also hardly ever any good (the present case is a happy exception). However, any scholar worth his salt knows the validity of the following statement: give me one great text, translated into English, rather than a thousand and one mediocre "original" texts (the ratio in our university's libraries is in reality more like 1,000,000 to 1). It goes without saying—and translators know this better than others—that as far as the ideas go, as a rule originals are more important to read than translations. Whatever the case, it is surely too early to tell whether the present work is a "great text": the gods—or rather, angels—that govern the intellectual spheres divulge their will only over long stretches of history. This does not mean that it does not expertly deal with a profound theme, and in a matchingly profound manner. It does. But it is only a sketch, and it is palpable to the reader that what he or she is observing in these lectures is someone's step to the side of his own philosophical/theological labors, a pause in order to catch his breath, to measure progress and to refocus on the task at hand. It is precisely this, a task, or rather, *the task*, that the author argues for and explores. The work in your hands is a translation of that work, or labor, of Jean-Yves Lacoste, and the translator had to inscribe himself—the best he could—into this work by, first, embracing the task. Such is the specific condition for the success of this translation, and its success can be partially measured by the translator's "hiddenness" and transparency I mentioned above. This minor "philosophy of translation" emerges embryonically, I think, from the work itself.

Despite its difficulty and thanklessness translation is serious intellectual work, and in this way it is rewarding work. These lectures were written with a light hand, I dare say an original and sophisticated style, which bids the reader to enter into a world of concepts mastered by a vast erudition in order to face a powerful argument. It packages, albeit inchoately and in cunningly simple language, the transition for Western reflection that it argues for: the "whole" of something very ancient but also very much alive is contained in what is nevertheless a small "fragment"—three fragments, to be precise, that compose one mounting argument involving a historical observation (with its implications) and a theoretical proposal. The "whole" of which I speak—however "fragmentarily" contained—is the Western religious and philosophical inheritance, nothing less.

A word is finally appropriate on the translation itself. The French language has a number of unique distinctions that present some difficulty in English. The most famous of these is probably that between *savoir* (knowledge, awareness, know-how) and *connaissance* (knowledge, understanding, expertise, consciousness), both of which in English can often be translated simply as "knowledge." The shorthand rule is that *savoir* is knowledge about, objective knowledge, whereas *connaissance*, from the verb *connaître*, has to do with acquaintance, that is, experiential knowledge. *Savoir* can also mean the totality of one's various kinds of knowledge, the content of one's erudition. Only *connaître*, however, is used in relation to people. As elsewhere in his work Lacoste uses this distinction with a clear philosophical intention, particularly in the second and third lectures here. A general awareness by the reader of the existence of this distinction in French is usually enough to guide them in discerning which word the English "knowledge" translates. When I judged that it is not, or for the sake of emphasis, I left the word in brackets. In one or two instances, I think, I translated *connaissance* as "understanding" and in another, as "experiential knowledge."

Lacoste also used another distinction in French, similar, perhaps, to a familiar one between *historique* and *historial*, that of *théologique* and *théologal*. This distinction mirrors the Latin and German distinctions, *theologale* and *theologicum* and *theologal* and *theologisch*, respectively. Both words are translated into modern English as "theological." (The English "theologal" is, according to the *OED*, now obsolete. However, it does appear in the 1994 American version of the *Catechism of the Catholic Church*.) In French, the "theological virtues" are *vertus théologales*, whereas "theological school" (for example) is *école théologique.* The French "théologal" (and its counterparts in other languages, including premodern English) is almost exclusively used in relation to faith, hope, and love, the "theological virtues." It has to do, then, with "infused" grace, personal participation in the life of God. In two instances, Lacoste presents the distinction. The catechism notwithstanding, I cut through the knot and replaced the phrase *théologique ou théologal* with "theological." Something is perhaps lost here, but if this is the case then it is simply lost in English altogether. This would not be the first time in the history of translation, in any case. One could use the term "theologal" and create an explanatory note, but I decided, for the sake of economy, simply to mention it here. In the first lecture in particular, Lacoste uses the terms "oeuvre" and "travail" in close proximity to one another. The French "oeuvre" can have a broader sense than it typically does as an English loanword, where it is almost exclusively delimited to a sole literary or artistic work or especially a collection of works, particularly by the same author. These terms can both be translated as "work" of course, which is the route I finally came to take. Besides aesthetic reasons, I did this for the specific reason that I wanted to keep the allusion that Lacoste makes in this context to the epigraph Heidegger once proposed for his collected works: "ways not works." Elsewhere, wherever I could, I used oeuvre in the familiar manner as a loanword. I almost always translated "travail" as "work" though I think occasionally as "labor" or "task." Finally, in the second lecture, Lacoste introduces the term *les spirituels* to describe a group of thinkers who had no place in the university, among either philosophers or theologians. "Spirituals" is a term in English, but used to describe a kind of early, religious folk music that developed in American slave communities. I translated Lacoste's term as "spiritual writers" or "spiritual authors." One loses the technicality of the term, but gains a good sense of who this group of thinkers was and what they did. Footnotes to the text by the translator are kept to a minimum and contained in brackets. The few words or phrases that were composed in English in the original are noted, unless a more pleasing solution presented itself, which it did on a few occasions. Thanks to Genevieve Fahey and to the members of Continental Philosophy Reading Group in Melbourne for their suggestions for improving this translation. It goes without saying that mistakes of varying degrees (always) remain, and these are solely due to the ineptitude of the translator himself.

I hope some of the flavor of this pleasurable, "Lacostian" French seeps through even my all too rocky attempt to render it into intelligible English. I hope, even more so, that the power of the argument remains intact. I hope hardly any less that the author of these lectures is pleased well enough with the tribute, both "hidden" (as much as possible) and laborious, that I offer as his translator. And, finally, for the reader: may the passage from theology to theological thinking for you be as demanding as enjoyable and as enjoyable as demanding here.

FROM THEOLOGY TO THEOLOGICAL THINKING

ONE

Theōria, vita philosophica, *and Christian Experience*

To give honor where honor is due, let the philosopher be the first to come on stage: after all, those whom we name "theologians" only adopted this label very late and, in the first centuries of Christianity, simply considered themselves philosophers. To make the gross distinction between "philosopher" and "theologian" is to be mistaken about the meaning of "philosophy" in the Greek and Greco-Roman world.[1] The first task imposed by the essence of the philosophical, or at least on any attempt to reach it, is to perplex the reader. Philosophy is not clearly defined, or better not defined at all. Yet a body of texts exists, which everyone agrees to call philosophical. (Similarly, it is universally agreed that certain others, the *Corpus Hermeticum*, for example, are not philosophical.) There were indeed some men whom everybody calls philosophers. But did they all play the same game? Was Socrates a philosopher in the same way as Plato or Aristotle after him? The perplexity promises to begin here. In order to express it, we are required to pass from one language to another and to wonder, not about what "theory" and "science" signify in our languages, but about what *theōria* and *epistēmē* mean in Greek. Philosophy began before Socrates, and we should stop calling "pre-Socratic" those who were philosophers in their own right and not mere precursors. We suggest that philosophy begins with the attempt to give an account of being [*l'étant*] in its totality—with theorizing about being in its totality. And *theōria* is not "theory" nor is *epistēmē* "science." There are certainly Heraclitean or Parmenidean theses, and many others. It would be ruinous, though, to conceive of them in light of the modern concept of theory. These theses speak of the totality of being, signified by words like *einai, phusis, noein,* etc. Yet they speak about it independently of all experimentation. And it should be observed that they are conceived a long time before a mathematization of the real is possible. At its dawn, philosophy seeks knowledge without being what we call science, or, more prudently, without sharing in the logic of what we call science. To speak of *theōria,* in Greek, whether in the "pre-Socratics" or after, is to name the contemplation of the real in its unfolding or budding forth. Assuredly, contemplation does not exclude conceptual knowledge: there is no philosophy without a proclivity for the concept. The *phusis* with which philosophy is occupied is not the *natura rerum:* reality as completed, accomplished, and at our disposal is unknown to it. The real which faces the philosopher appears to him in its bursting forth; his ambition is to perceive the subterranean reasons which preside over this bursting forth that he is unable to master. And it is quite possible that we still have something to learn from the (always salubrious) critique of the "nature of things" by *phusis.*

Here we meet the Socratic moment in the history of philosophy, or, more precisely, the Socratic moment of philosophy. Socrates, who wrote nothing, and whom we know from the written traces of his words, has imparted to us some philosophemes and/or some philosophical lessons. About the nature of things, however, he says nothing: only the being that we are matters to him. And if we admit that there is no philosophy without a philosopher, which we are authorized to do here, even if the philosophical text, when there is one, matters incomparably more than its author (after all, it happens that we often have to read anonymous or pseudonymous texts . . .), it would be necessary to admit that Socrates figures first, or nearly first, in making the work of philosophy (and all its dialectical exigencies) and the life of the philosopher coincide.

Long after Socrates, Heidegger will say that the only biography of the philosopher is the list of his written works. Husserl, for his part, considered the philosopher to be a "Functionary of Mankind."² Socratic experience cannot accommodate itself to these two positions. Socrates is a practitioner of *theōria*, though restricted to a contemplation of man and not things (his work is therefore less ambitious than the "theoretical praxis" which Husserl talks about occasionally, and which seeks to turn its attention to the whole of the *onta*). Yet Socrates does not play the role of philosopher without playing other roles as well (that of citizen, for example), but his role as philosopher encompasses all the others: he is a philosopher and lives in philosophy, which exceeds all functionalism. And if his life overlaps precisely with his philosophical teaching, then his philosophy is a "lived philosophy." Here we do not escape from a difficult hermeneutical task—that of reading the work starting from the life and the life starting from the work. Subsequently the Cynics will furnish a caricature of the *vita philosophica*—but the caricature, if it is so unilateral (the Cynic wants to lead a "philosophical life" but dispenses with the work of *theōria*), truly gives us much to think about. To live philosophically—this is what Socrates accomplishes in a way that is as resolute as it is decisive. His work is what Plato and Xenophon have transmitted from his conversations, and we are free to seek a "Socrates of history" masked in part by the Socrates of his students. His work, however, forms part of an action, the principle of which is that of rendering philosophy coextensive with life. This negates the reduction of the philosopher to his works, a principle affirmed by Heidegger. Philosophical action rather than philosophical work; philosophy as irreducible to any profession; the philosopher as antagonist, therefore, to the sophist. What Socrates teaches (but Kierkegaard opportunely reminds us that Socrates teaches nothing), he lives. The etymology tells us that the philosopher is a lover of wisdom. Socrates seeks the wise life, and he holds on to the language of love. He will pursue the quest for the wise life up to his death. This does not suggest that the philosophical life condemns one to persecution (nor that the philosophical word is devoted to it). But it does suggest indeed that the one who lives the life of a philosopher ought not fail to die the death of a philosopher . . .

Nothing allows us to say that the "pre-Socratics" did not live as philosophers, nor that this ceased to be the case in Plato and Aristotle: Heidegger has demonstrated that for them philosophy is a way of existing.[3] The intervention of these two in the history of philosophy no less marks a turn. Geometry is necessary for the student of Plato. Aristotle's physics is a metaphysics, but his logic is a definitive contribution to science, and his biology a contribution long since outdated, though it merits not being forgotten by historians. Having said that, we ought to be at liberty to say that what classifies as *theōria* in Socratism and before Socrates—the contemplation of the whole of being or of the being that we are—will, from now on, in many areas of philosophy but certainly not all, classify as "theory" in the modern sense of the term. This allows Husserl, in §12 of the *Crisis*, to leap over the centuries in order to define the Greek origins of the scientific project in modern terms. We could always suggest that every scientific work (we will return to the question of what "science" means and does not mean) has its contemplative or reverential moment, and we would be right to do so. Science is not reduced to the reign of technology. But this matters little here. By effecting a certain return to the ambitions of pre-Socratic thought, Plato and Aristotle redouble this return by a recourse to an a priori and geometric construction of the cosmos (Plato) or to its description grounded on rudimentary experimentation tied to some a priori schemes (Aristotle),[4] in such a way that philosophy can then be practiced without being ipso facto a form of moral life: *sophia* does not mean "wisdom" but supreme knowledge.[5] Thus we must accept that there was a transition from *theōria* to theory. *Theōria* was certainly not totally other than theory. The distance from the *bios theōretikos* to Husserl's "theoretical attitude" was nevertheless greater than what is incontestably the right to theory present in *theōria* and cannot be totally separated from it. Was the development of theory out of *theōria* a blessing or a curse? Let us prudently refrain from taking a position.

The scientific theories of Aristotle, first and foremost the foundation of the logic of propositions, are contributions to knowledge and are only secondarily philosophical "theories." The cosmogony of the *Timaeus*, on the other hand, gives us no knowledge about the cosmos that it builds a priori (in fact the demiurge is more important than the product of its demiurgy), but it provides much knowledge about the philosophy of Plato (about the Platonic manner of doing philosophy), even, and perhaps above all, when it is shown incapable of envisaging the universe from a point of view that we would call scientific. In both cases, and all differences set aside, a movement is inaugurated (or revived) after Socratism, and in this movement, what must be seen, on the one hand, is the annexation of all knowledge by philosophy and, on the other hand, the quasi bracketing of the "philosophical life" in favor of a "wise" life defined as access to the highest knowledge. Henceforth the sage is defined as the one who knows and not as the one who leads the "good life," or, if we accept Heidegger's interpretation, as the one who grasps the highest possibility of existence, which is the highest knowledge. Certainly in Plato the philosopher has the vocation of being king, since he will reign with virtue, and with more virtue than the non-philosopher. And it is in complete agreement with his moral and political philosophy that Plato, falling short of becoming a king, will counsel a tyrant. Again, the philosopher in Aristotle is admirably placed to fill the role of tutor to a prince, whom he can dream of teaching to reign virtuously. Someone learning the logic of Aristotle, however, does not find there a school of wisdom but of *sophia*, and someone seeking in Plato a theory of the production of the universe will find it there, but does not find it tied to any art of living. One does not have the thoughtlessness to pass by in silence the moral philosophy of Plato and Aristotle, especially in a time of Aristotelian revival. The philosophy of both thinkers knows how to make room for an *ars vivendi*. But the possession of this art is not required in order to read the *Parmenides* or the *Metaphysics*, no more than it has one of its sources in this reading. Philosophy is presented in the guise of an art of reasoning. The one who reasons evidently participates in the game of life. Yet this game is not necessarily ethical. The moral competencies of the philosopher can be limited. And it is a cause of some disquiet to invoke the figure of the immoral philosopher and, who knows, the immoral moralist.

Let me hasten to say that these cursory reminders neither want nor are able to break every link between *theōria* and theorization, between philosophical life and philosophical work. And for the breaking point, we can provide for ourselves an issue lying outside the quandary indicated above, which has only a preliminary value. Thus, a thesis, and some glosses: philosophy is to be understood as a work or as a way of life; in any case, to philosophize is a manner of being in the world. This is understood in many ways: (a) Philosophy is first a human affair. We have the right to suppose that dolphins are persons; we have the right to speculate about the intelligence of unreachable inhabitants of the farthest galaxies, but we cannot attribute to either an aptitude for philosophy and its exercise, unless we adopt a naive anthropomorphism (the "philosophy" of dolphins and Martians is perhaps better than ours but what do we mean here by "better"?). The use of intelligence is not a disposition toward philosophy. The angels and demons are more intelligent than we are, but what questions do they pose? Dolphins and Martians are perhaps more intelligent than we are, but perhaps they possess an innate practice of wisdom that dispenses them from research—their "philosophy" does not coincide with ours. Evidently, this ought to be clarified. Philosophy is a human affair without being an affair of every man. Every man eats, drinks, and sleeps, or uses tools, we all speak or chatter, but not everyone attends to the work of philosophy—just as not all are painters or sculptors. (But we can propose to all a vulgarized version of Aristotle's ethics, or of any other moral philosophy, and rightly suppose that the choice of the "good life" is not the concern of the philosopher alone . . .) I propose a second clarification: All are not poets, nor are all philosophers. Yet philosophy occupies a privileged place in the midst of every human activity for the good reason that it alone is able to live and, together with it, to think about what it does. The poet probably lives what he writes, but this is the case for any human activity that implies an element of self-involvement (and it is rare that we do not enfold ourselves in what we do). However, the poet lives in the world like everyone else, even if he often enjoys a sharpened experience of being in the world; to write poetry is a way of being in the world that no major phenomenological disjunction distinguishes from the works of the painter, architect, or laborer; there are definitely differences but there is no rupture. The poet certainly tells us often about his (experience of the) world, and perhaps even tells us how his poetic work gives him access to the phenomena of the world. Yet for all that, does the poet think the world? He often *speaks* the world better than the philosophers say it. But regarding what he says better, does it not follow that he dispenses with concepts? Poetry reflects the phenomena of the world a little better than every other human work or experience, but the questions of the philosopher are not those of the poet (and the poet may very well not pose questions at all). It was one of the great merits of Heidegger to have examined in detail the coexistence of the philosopher and the poet, which is, in any case, a major fact. The philosopher sometimes expresses himself poetically (Parmenides, Lucretius). The philosopher (Heidegger, again) has been capable of learning from the poet. Nevertheless, the philosopher is the one in the world who poses what we could call the "question of the world." How is the world as such different from the cosmos, the earth, or the universe? Only the philosopher, in the plurality of philosophical traditions, is the bearer of this question. And we must say that he is the one in the world who reflects on his being-in-the-world. Here and now, he is the one not content to live this here and this now, but who reflects on them or, to put it vaguely, who "thinks" them. It matters little to the present remarks whether he thinks them well or poorly: it is sufficient for us that the world appears as a problem, and being-in-the-world along with it (why are we in the world and not free with regard to it?), to everyone who makes a profession out of seeking after wisdom. Certain thinkers have done it without knowing it.[6] We can no longer allow ourselves to be ignorant of it; if we did, we would be deceived about the nature of philosophy. (b) A philosophical path ought then to be considered as leading philosophy to its outermost limit and as exceeding the Greek ambitions of philosophy, that of every philosophy [sic] which aims to liberate man from his humanity or allows him to transcend it. We possess the near perfect example of such an attempt in the works of the first Fink, whether the *Sixth Cartesian Meditation* or the posthumous fragments from the same period. The transcendental reduction—or so affirms Husserl's last assistant with his imprudent blessing—can preside over the genesis of a new humanity (which is conceived easily in Husserlian terms, since the reduction requires a radical conversion), and above all liberate us from our humanity by liberating us from our being-in-the-world (Husserl himself, however, cannot say this, because the transcendental reduction takes place in the lifeworld, to which we will always be subject). Here phenomenology deviates in the direction of a rather disturbing gnosis (which gnosis is not?) in which a dehumanized or overhumanized *ego* (which the "impartial spectator" of *Ideas* I is not) becomes ipso facto nonexistent or something other than existent. This should be nuanced. The pathos of existence, as it issued from Heidegger, made a disagreeable sound in Husserl's ears. It is obvious that for Husserl philosophy is a "science" in both a Germanic and a modern sense (and probably more Germanic—*Wissenschaft*—than modern) and that its link to *theōria* is reduced to the extreme. In any case the "impartial spectator" or the "transcendental I" is surpassed by the work of the reduction and also known only when, this work accomplished, one returns to the quotidian gestures of being-in-the-world, or rather—to be more Husserlian—by naive contact with the lifeworld. Phenomenological "praxis" intends to be as scientific as possible, and just about the only truly scientific activity, the pure and simple holder of the foundations of all science, but if there is a time to practice science, there is also a time to be delivered over to cares with no scientific pretension: it is not from his waking moment to his falling asleep that the philosopher is a "functionary of humanity," but, more modestly, during the time that he consecrates to philosophy (this certainly does not prohibit him from being a philosopher from the time he wakes up to the time he goes to bed, of which Husserl's use of time provides the perfect example). But in the excesses of Fink these quotidian cares, by which man manifests that he is a man and not an angel or separated intelligence, lose all true weight. Philosophy is no longer a truly human enterprise (only the decision to philosophize, in the strict sense, is human). The philosopher as philosopher (once the transcendental reduction is accomplished) is no longer truly human. And it would be necessary to admit that a rupture emerges between Husserl and Fink which separates philosophy from what we have called gnosis. The word does not appear by chance. *Gnosis*, under the canonical forms that it assumed in late antiquity, proposed to save (by knowledge, *gnōsis*, therefore) by delivering from the world. The knowledge that it proposed did not lead to a well-being in the world: it was a way of taking leave of the world. The objection raised against Fink could doubtlessly be raised against other philosophies. It is raised against Fink, however, to the degree that what he describes—the phenomenological advent of a more than humanity—well and truly reflects an experience of the world. Of the world such as one wants to leave it and not as one wants it to be or knows it should be. Of the world, therefore, as the milieu of Gnostic experience. (c) Philosophical *work* and philosophical *life* do not necessarily overlap, and it is worth making a choice between them. It is certain, however, that they can overlap and the philosopher can live as a philosopher. Whether we speak of Socrates or of his predecessors and successors, the centuries of Greek and Latin philosophy (to mention only them) bear witness to the permanent possibility of a *vita philosophica*. The affirmation that the philosopher lives life itself, on the one hand, and that he ought to live as a philosopher, on the other (which distinguishes him crucially from the sophist), is maintained throughout Greece and Rome. The mathematician cannot form the project of living a "mathematical life," a *vita mathematica:* the concept would be absurd. (And it is not certain that the possession of moral virtues is useful for mathematical work . . .) The mathematician can certainly live for mathematics, like the musician can for music. Yet the philosopher is not only the one who lives for philosophy but the one who is able to live philosophically; and this possibility, as one chooses, is that which is perceived as a duty or ought to be perceived as such. If, to do the work of philosophy, it were sufficient to sit down and calculate (one will pardon me for leaping over the centuries to evoke the Leibnizian project), then our manner of working would not (necessarily) step into a manner of living. However, Greece did not know the idea of conceptual calculus, even if it bequeathed us the first rudiments of logic. And not knowing it, that is, knowing philosophy as *epistēmē* and not as science, a constraint weighed on it: not to envisage philosophy as a profession that one practices for fixed hours, though if/where necessary to earn one's livelihood, but letting the philosophical project integrally take over the philosopher's life. The philosopher assuredly wants to know and is given the means. He evidently has time for the work of the concept: the "science" that he practices must make a place for some technical skill. He is a man of *theōria;* he is also a producer of what we call theories. But another Greek word ought to be uttered here, but not in order to know what *theōria* involves: *ethos.*

The affirmation that philosophy in its ancient form is both "theoretical" and "ethical" is as trite as it is fundamental. Philosophy wants to know and it inseparably wants to live the "good life," of which it has the means to do so. (The life devoted to knowing has a strong chance of being the "good life.") The popularized philosophy of the Hellenistic world, then that of late antiquity, both demonstrate this with complete purity as well as a share of exaggeration. Philosophy is already "popular" in Socrates, all the more so in what receives after him the name of "popular philosophy." We do not need to be snobbish about such a philosophy, reduced to a moral *eros* or to some elementary principles about the *phusis*, and formulated in such a way as to be appropriable or at least understandable by all. Stoicism becomes impoverished in its late form where it is reduced to an ethics that brackets any interest in "physics" or logic. However, the impoverishment has the merit of enhancing a moment, the ethical moment, without which philosophy is simply found denatured or dehumanized. By the pen of a slave or emperor, Epictetus or Marcus Aurelius, we find only some platitudes of Stoic morals. The theoretical insufficiency of such texts cannot mask the lesson they give more or less despite themselves. Popular philosophy teaches us that the art of thinking and the art of living cannot (or ought not) be separated. If we accept the lessons offered by popular philosophy, the ideal of the philosophical life necessarily includes the possession of the art of thinking, just as much as the art of thinking is essentially tied to the art of living. Late Stoicism and the popular philosophy of the empire have little theoretical vigor. And it is unfortunate that no serious contribution to philosophy emerged from them. Their conception of the philosophical, however, has some merit: leading us back to an essential trait of philosophy or a primordial philosophical *pathos* without which philosophy is condemned to take the path before it, where *theōria* and *ethos* are reduced to the profit of a solely theoretical work, the path that leads it to the position that it occupies in the scientific visions of the world—and at the end of this path the ethical disappears, the *phusis* is handed over to the cares of physical science; logic alone remains. *Logos* alone remains, then, and it is no longer anything but the *logos* of logic and of the surveillance that it exercises over scientific procedures. All philosophy faithful to its origins ought to protest against its reduction to the state of *Wissenschaft:* its proper rigor does not have to be that of the sciences, even if it ought not to be any less.

It is finally possible for us to introduce the intrusion of Christianity onto the intellectual scene of late antiquity. By the pen of Christian authors (Paul of Tarsus, Tertullian, etc.) as well as pagan (Celsus, Porphyry, etc.) this intrusion could pass as that of the irrational, first of all as the "folly" of the cross, in the field of the rational. There is however a misunderstanding on both sides. The Greek philosopher does not perceive the omnipresence of the *logos* in Christian discourse, beginning with the divine *logos* and, therefore, with the paradoxical *logos* of the cross. The Christian author, likewise, does not always see how indebted he is to Hellenism and its ways of reasoning. Two points should be insisted upon here. (a) One cannot emphasize too much the roots that Christianity plunged into a Judaism that we know was strongly Hellenized at the time of the first announcements of the Gospel.[7] Antiphilosophism was certainly present and virulent: the Haggadah, among others, contains some traces of polemic against a (Greek) *logos* not indigenous to Israel. Hellenistic Judaism did not ask about being, nor evidently why there was something rather than nothing (but these questions are also absent from the popular philosophies of the empire and it is not absolutely certain any longer that they have to be posed in order for it to be philosophy). However, it asks about the good life in terms similar to the philosophies of its time. The set of texts of the New Testament that we are absolutely certain were written in Greek, the Pauline corpus, betray some minor, but incontestable, philosophical competencies. Well before Paul, the sapiential literature had arisen in a Judaism that Greece had invaded in the person of Alexander. And a little before Paul, the work of Philo had rendered clear witness to a possible alliance between Judaism and Hellenism. When Christianity is introduced as a third, any direct opposition between Judaism and Hellenism ought therefore to be squarely refused. (b) The earliest Christian preaching proposes a *logos* that belongs neither to Judaism nor to philosophy: the "word" of the cross, or its proper rationality, *logos tou staurou*. The effect of this *logos* is to scandalize (the Jew) or drive mad (the Greek)—and it is not necessary to say anything further. However, it is necessary to admit that it really is a matter of a *logos*, of a word that renders intelligible, and that if the scandal was destined to remain, the Christian soon stopped wearing the vestments of the fool (non-sage) in order to don those of the one who deserves, according to the lexical usages of the late empire, to pass for a philosopher. In Paul, and later in Tertullian and others, Christianity certainly appears as a non-philosophy. But in the long run its destiny was that its "logic" featured among the logics of all the living philosophies of that epoch (that of Platonism in the first place)—up to the point that in Theodoret Hellenism appears to the Christian as "sick" and rationally deficient. Let us insist that to oppose "theology" and "philosophy" is anachronistic if we want to describe an intellectual passage where there was simply a debate between rational animals and where the true dispute was not, for example, about knowing or believing, but between one figure of rationality and another, between a discourse that wants to be seen as true and another discourse that wants the same. (One can perhaps add here that the opposition of the Greek—therefore of the philosopher— and the barbarian is refused from the beginning by Christianity. This refusal implicitly prohibits the Christian from being party to any barbarity whatsoever. This does not mean that the first words pronounced by the Christians for the attention of the Greeks were not dedicated to passing as barbaric, above all the proclamation of a salvation intended for the body . . .) Let us not forget as well that the distinction between the "natural" and "supernatural" was at this time unknown, thus depriving the Christian of a facile immunization strategy and obligating him to speak with the Greek as an equal. The Christian experience, as rigorously announced from before the final redaction of the evangelical texts, concerns knowledge. The Christian is a man of gnosis. Among men capable of knowledge, a debate is always possible. Therefore, described as a third people beside those who adhere to the Mosaic law and those who seek Greek wisdom, Christianity was destined also to appear (and to appear to itself) as proposing a wisdom and a love of wisdom.

Alongside the common love of "gnosis," however, the difference of worldview must be taken into account. The comparison of the worlds of Celsus and Origen, already made a long time ago under the direction of Harnack, remains illuminating.[8] We live, perhaps, if Habermas is to be believed, in the age of post-secularization.[9] Yet here we are overcrowded by concepts, prejudices, and mentalities that were the work of a secularization about which it is better not to believe, or to assert for that matter, that we have definitively left it behind. We have for a long time upheld the duty of consecrating the memory of the *Lumières* and of what they built or destroyed (as one chooses)— and if the post-secularization that concerns the later Habermas allows the peaceable coexistence of religious man and secularized man, it is better not to believe too quickly that a problem has disappeared and that secularization no longer maintains any other pretension than of being tolerated like it tolerates the religious rationalities. Classic and late antiquity, on the other hand, itself possessed an anticipated experience of the Enlightenment: the paganism of Proclus is a demythologized version of what the pagans of former centuries believed (supposing they did believe it). But what matters to us here is that the cosmos, though demythologized by the philosophers, did not cease for all that (for the philosophers, non-philosophers, and Christian thinkers alike) to be the setting for bringing the divine or the sacred into play. In Neoplatonism there is something like a pagan salvation history. The face-to-face opposition of Christianity and paganism (on a double front: the one where a strict monotheism is opposed to polytheism and to the henologies, and the one where the "word of the cross" is presented as a critique of every other word) does not exclude some commonalities of belief, whether implicit or explicit. Atheism is unknown to antiquity (the Greco-Roman world probably knew only one coherent atheist, Lucretius). When it takes place, the pagan-Christian polemic is not about the possibility of a divine intrusion into the world of men, but rather the modalities of this intrusion. Had the divine *logos*, familiar to the Jew Philo, as well as to Middle Platonism and Neoplatonism, pitched its tent in a Jew from Nazareth and in him alone? There is nothing in the thesis that the gods visit men at will to which paganism, whether of the people or of the philosophers, was compelled to raise objections. Paganism totally conceded to Christianity that there are demons and angels, that the cosmos is not only the stage for a drama played out among men and only men. It was also conceded without hesitation that the divine has to be not only confirmed but also celebrated with piety—in the empire a *religio licita* is not a tolerated belief but a tolerated cult. The stumbling block is the Christian or Judeo-Christian exclusivism—*Absolutheitsanspruch*. The scandal is twofold. First, that a crucified man can receive the title of God. Second, that he alone, along with the one who sent him, can lawfully bear the titles that Christianity recognizes in him. A crucified who is God; a crucified who alone is God: the religious syncretism of late paganism can evidently only see this as a provocation. All agree that the sacred is there, that the divine exists, that there is a numinous, that divine messengers exist (and divine messages, whether of the Oracle at Delphi or the counsels given by Asclepius to Aelius Aristides). However, Christianity's rationality is not that of a divine and its diffusion throughout the whole world, but that of a Christological concentration, or a revelation concentrated in a Middle Eastern fragment of history and in it alone. And the vision of the world that the pagans and Christians more or less held in common during the first centuries of Christianity will pass to the background without ever completely disappearing (there will always remain a residual paganism in Christianity), as and when Christianity imposes that which in its worldview is unacceptable to paganism (and to the degree that it gives a vision of the world that measures up to what it believes).

The world is common to us all: this belongs to its phenomenological definition. Some worldviews can intersect. The problem of the clash between Christianity and paganism was therefore not truly there. If the *logos* is as common as being-in-the-world, the battle is about versions or modes of the *logos*; and between the pagan and Christian versions, the break was necessarily greater than any proximity. Despite the "preparations of the Gospel" that the goodwill of the Church Fathers was so quick to identify, Christianity could only smash to pieces the pagan relation to the world, and even subvert the most demythologized versions of paganism—hence Pseudo-Dionysius's exemplary subversion of the cosmos of Proclus. What these two visions or images of the world had in common, appearing clearly in Celsus's *True Discourse* and in Origen's replica of it, was inevitably erased when Christianity, pursuing the work of Judaism, appears in fact as an agent of secularization, its doctrine of creation requiring (and authorizing) the establishment of the cleanest break possible between the divine and non-divine sphere. Not only are the angels of Christianity only angels, but even the gods of paganism are only (fallen) angels. "Only": the Christian will have to ask if his place within the marketplace of the "post-secular" city is truly in the camp of religious men who converse courteously with secularized man.

In speaking of Proclus we have departed from Christian origins on the one hand, and on the other we have discouraged the belief in an easy triumph of the Christian *logos*. The philosophers were prohibited from staying in the empire and fled to Persia. This banishment proves that they still existed under their pagan identity until the time of Justinian. His closing of the Academy in 539 first possesses symbolic value—pagan reason no longer has the right of citizenship in the city—but let there be no mistake: it is also the closing of a truly living school. Well, alive albeit scarce for some time. And when Neoplatonism cast its last rays over the horizon the Christian ways of reasoning remained from Byzantium to Rome the only ones that deserved (or solicited) assent. From this point the figure of the pagan philosopher becomes anachronistic.

The assent solicited by Christianity was threefold. First it was the assent required by a philosophy that had prevailed over all others. It was also the assent demanded by a religious or cultural universe that had swept aside that of paganism. Finally, last but not least,[10] a consent to a style of life—to a new form of "philosophical life." (a) It was more or less a common idea, since Justin, that Christianity was not a non-philosophy but realized the aspirations of the philosopher, without there being a complete break between a purely philosophical rationality (for where does one find philosophy in its pure state?) and this rationality that still does not yet bear the name of "theology." From the time of a notion that was a tiny bit outrageous in Clement of Alexandria, it was also a near universal opinion that (pagan) philosophy was a sort of third Testament destined for the Greeks and having the value of an "evangelical preparation."[11] Justin, Clement, and Origen spoke to the philosophers, or about them, without themselves possessing great philosophical competence. (Though Origen was perhaps the co-disciple of Plotinus at the school of Ammonius Saccas.)[12] The name of Marius Victorinus ought to be mentioned after theirs, the first philosopher of any stature to have embraced Christianity and, after his conversion, to have brought about a contribution of the same stature to Christian doctrine (above all to Trinitarian theology). For his part, Augustine was pushed to Christianity among other reasons by reading, in Latin translation, the "Platonic books," though we are not sure which ones specifically. But after the extinction of Greek and pagan Neoplatonism, the Christian books no longer need to lean on the Platonic books and no longer have the mission, even marginally, of refuting whatever these books contain that is unacceptable to Christianity. Henceforth Plato is a "Plato christianus." Stoicism, meanwhile, will survive within Christianity in a fragmentary form in order to reappear much later in the influence its ethic will exercise beginning in the Renaissance. Finally, Aristotle will be almost completely forgotten until his medieval "entrance" into the West. Maximus the Confessor was probably the lone Father to manifest some debt to him. Thus it was that Christianity, from the seventh century on, comes out as representative and near sole defender of rationality and therefore at base as dominant philosophy. The history that leads to the triumph of the Christian *logos* over the pagan *logos* is well known, whatever one's interpretation of it. (b) Speaking in purely philosophical terms is insufficient. The fact is that the originality of Neoplatonism was in being a religious philosophy: not only a philosophy interested in religious phenomena but even a philosophy that led to certain religious or quasi-religious practices. Beyond their theoretical texts, the Neoplatonists have their Bible, the Chaldean Oracles, slightly predating the foundation of the school.[13] Not only do they have their own theology, *expressis verbis*, but they also possess their own rites. The witnesses regarding the practice of theurgy, the animation of statues, etc., are not numerous but are undeniably conclusive. Assuredly, Neoplatonic religiosity is a pagan piety rewritten for the learned. When Proclus arrives in Athens and makes his devotions on the Acropolis, those who rejoice about it see in him a young neoconservative, but it is an ancient ancestor of Bultmann with whom they are dealing. We must insist however that the disassociation of traditional religion and philosophy, probably an operation as old as philosophy itself, did not deprive Greek philosophy of every link with Greek religiosity. And it is certainly lexically anachronistic but not aberrant at all to propose that Proclus, in the *Platonic Theology* or the *Elements*, wanted to elevate to the level of concept that which the majority of still pagan Greeks believed under the mode of representation. When Christianity establishes itself, in the East and West, it does so by replacing a simultaneously philosophical and theological universe: Christianity is inextricably a new philosophy and a new theology. (c) From this we conclude that, once the contemplative and theoretical tasks of pagan philosophy have become those of "Christian philosophy," the existential tasks once tied to the work of pagan philosophy cannot miss undergoing a similar transformation. When pagan philosophy is no longer there, we are not attending to a collapse of philosophy as such. Here Christian experience is dedicated to taking the reins of the *vita philosophica*. Or dedicated to proving that it had taken the reins from its beginning . . .

Regarding the (multiple) tasks that devolve upon Christianity, and in order to understand that the philosophical life and Christian life have become synonymous, it is necessary to go further. We just said that a philosophy, "Christian philosophy," in the sense that Augustine gave to the syntagm, establishes itself through the course of the centuries over every other philosophy, and that a religious universe is superimposed upon that of late paganism. This needs to be clarified. The survival of paganism within Neoplatonism was accomplished at the cost of a reinterpretation. But the Christianity that imposed little by little its ways of reasoning during this period had hardly any need for the reinterpretation or revision of its sources: never does allegory mask the letter and its truth. It is probably not necessary any more to refute Harnack, not least because he ignores the degree to which the Greek spirit is already present in the foundational texts of Christianity. Neoplatonism has its scriptures, as we have mentioned, and Christianity has its own as well. Yet the parallelism disappears when we note that Christianity always observes a scrupulous fidelity with respect to its foundational texts. (The influence of the Chaldean Oracles on Neoplatonism is real but textually marginal, whereas recourse to the biblical text in the Christian writings is perpetual.) Christianity, of course, equips itself with hermeneutics. For Origen, scripture is given to the simple as well as to the learned, but a sense is accessible only to the wise, the spiritual sense, which remains hidden to the simple (as long as the wise do not give them the key . . .). However, between the literal sense and spiritual or allegorical sense, no division could separate the wise and simple from one another. Before Origen, Clement of Alexandria distinguished the man who lives the "simple" faith, the so-called Pistic, and the believer in possession of a plenitude of knowledge, the Gnostic. But even in this case what distinguishes the haves from the have-nots is not an esoteric knowledge blocked off from the exoteric knowledge of the letter of the texts, but a knowledge more or less found in the ecstasy derived from the same truth. From these examples (which could be supported by reference to the Antiochene exegesis and its steady desire to maintain the primacy of the literal sense) one can conclude easily that if Christianity comes in the end to appear as the dominant religious philosophy of its time, it is without doubt as a learned discourse, though first perhaps under the guise of a popular philosophy—knowledge given to all and wisdom practicable by all. Christian *theōria* is evidently associated with specific Christian theories, which are not always enunciated in popular form. The monks of the Egyptian desert had not read the theoretical writings of Athanasius, their first propagandist. But—and it is precisely here that Christianity takes the reins of the pagan philosophies, whether scholarly or popular—the art proposed by Christianity is inseparably an art of knowing and an art of living, an art of knowing bound up in an art of living intended for all. Stoicism proposed to its adherents an *ethos*, that of life lived in conformity with the *phusis*. Christianity proposes its own. And Christianity, for want of being founded on "nature," is founded on the revelatory meaning of a fragment of history. It makes a theory about this meaning and opposes it to pagan rationality. However, the theory or theories that it proposes are first *theōria*, and *theōria* includes leading to an *ethos*. The "theoretical" ought to be lived. And in living it the Christian rejoins with the *eros* that animated the Greek and Roman philosophies for which in some manner it has substituted itself. "Christian life" and "philosophical life" coincide therefore when Christianity is almost the sole occupier of the intellectual scene of the empire. To state this more prudently: for lack of other concepts, Christian experience gives itself to be understood as "philosophical life."

Let us try to illuminate a little more the ethical character of Christian *theōria*, or the style given in Christianity to the union of the "theoretical" and the ethical. We have not spoken of a Christian *praxis* (this could easily have been done by drawing attention to the life and organization of the first communities and to the concrete details furnished by the Pauline corpus, for example). The richer concept of *praktikē* ought to retain our attention. The term comes to us from the monastic milieu of Egypt and is commonly associated with the name of Evagrius Ponticus, perhaps the sole solitary of the Egyptian desert to have been an intellectual. By *praktikē* monastic spirituality understood *ascesis*, the prelude to the pure contemplation of God. In the first place the monk is thus defined by what he "does" or by his "deeds." And, distinguishing him from every philosophical school (the mysticism of Evagrius is an intellectualism that owes practically nothing to philosophical influences), what he does surely assigns to him the status of philosopher. This is confirmed by his own words and agrees with the intellectual climate of his day. His theoretical and conceptual competency is generally poor. But this weakness does not prohibit him, when he articulates it himself, from being the successor to those who desired to live a "philosophical life" (and of appearing thus when one speaks of him). In a time when the sacrificial cults have disappeared,[14] and when the men of God, the *holy men*, are the locus of attraction for a new piety,[15] the monk is the one from whom his brothers can seek a word of salvation—*lege moi rhēma pōs sōthō*—and who can provide them with a response. The theme of monastic life as philosophical life or as the new face of philosophical life has been developed by Hans Urs von Balthasar in a magisterial article that discloses the conditions by which we can speak without contradiction of "Christian philosophy."[16] In appearance the monk resides in proximity to a well-known (though theoretically unproductive) philosophical current, Cynicism. Only in appearance, however. He distances himself from the Cynic, in fact, and from all popular philosophy along with him, by withdrawing from the city (leaving it to transform the desert into a city peopled by anchorites alone).[17] The agora where free men debate philosophical questions is a place where he refuses to appear (and which hardly exists any longer), even if, as for the Cynics, he ought to speak there only by gestures or parabolic actions. This does not prohibit philosophy from including the anchorite, nor does it prohibit it from incorporating every philosophical alternative. At the end of his study, Balthasar draws attention to a more contemporary example: Edith Stein leaving the philosophical and university life for the cloister. Can the Carmelite life be considered a "philosophical life"? Let us set aside the question of the value of Stein's philosophical texts before her conversion to Christianity or after her conversion to Neo-Thomism (their reading rarely excites enthusiasm and her best work remains her doctoral thesis, which proposes a non-Husserlian treatment of the concept of *Einfühlung*), for the essential lies somewhere else. It can be found in her taking leave of professional philosophy, an act itself worthy of being called philosophical; and this taking leave causes us to consider the dialectic of continuity and discontinuity which, if we understood aright, manifests precisely in what sense the monk or nun can be called a philosopher, and perhaps even more of a philosopher, more of a lover of wisdom, than the (indispensable) producers of philosophical theories. The monk can be called philosopher because he *lives* that which the philosopher ought to desire: perpetual attention to the most important, despite everything that can divert us from it. Thus the monk forces us never to forget that philosophy is an alliance of a *theōria* and a *praxis*, for him, a *praktikē*. This *theōria* certainly depends on theories, the conceptual nuances of which the monk will master well or poorly, though it is not required of him to possess more than the simple *credo* of every believer. But in the same way as the martyr, whom he has the ambition of succeeding at a time when, in the empire, nobody has to spill his blood for Christ any longer, the monk is the bearer of a witness which has the value of teaching it. His experience, which can legitimately pass as a "lived theology," can be termed in Greek both *bios theōretikos* and *bios philosophikos*. The monk lives the life that merits being lived, and that merits being lived because he is jealously faithful to the highest Good.

This suffices to confer on him the dignity of philosopher. This is the case in late antiquity certainly. And in other times, why not?

It would be rash to idealize here. The monastic project is one thing (as are those who resemble it) and its realization is another. In the Benedictine tradition, the first thing that the postulant asks of the community of which he seeks to be a member is the *conversio morum*. The monk aspires to what the Eastern tradition names the "angelic life," but his aspiration is that of a sinner, of a friend of wisdom who is even so not a wise man. The monk wants to set up camp to the side of the "world," of the "age," but the experience of the desert is inevitably one of being-in-the-world. Whether we understand the world in its New Testament sense or phenomenological sense, we only leave it through death. It is manifestly the same for the pagan philosopher to whom we suggest that the monk is the successor. Marsilius Ficino prays to "Saint Socrates" with every appearance of reason, but what other philosopher could one pray to with such confidence? We know that one can be a great philosopher without being a saint. Worse, we know that one can be a great theologian without being one. Examples abound.[18] Barth and Tillich (for whom, certainly, theology knows no other holiness but God's own . . .) were not saints. Cyril of Alexandria even less so. There are morally respectable philosophers: Husserl, Wittgenstein in his own way, and, in all likelihood, Kierkegaard. Mentioning them, a little higgledy-piggledy, allows us to introduce two qualifications: On the one hand, some accurate theories can be the work of theoreticians who do not live a truly "philosophical" life. On the other hand, passion for *theōria*, or more simply the leading of a truly philosophical/theological *life*, does not guarantee the accuracy of theories. On the one hand, the monk is morally fallible, and the philosopher just as much. On the other hand, and almost worst, the saint can flirt with heterodoxy: the Marian theology of Maximilian Kolbe is Christian (and Catholic) only in an expanded sense, and in making ample use of the principle of charity in his regard.

Here we touch the weak point of another good article by Balthasar, consecrated to "theology and sanctity."[19] We do not deny that the saints make a contribution to theology by their very style of life—if the monk lives the *vita philosophica*, his life can be a lesson in philosophy for all, and for Christians a lesson in theology. Here's the rub: the fact remains that theological genius (or at least theological talent) pertains to the domain of "charism," to *gratia gratis data*, and not to "sanctifying grace," *gratia gratum faciens*. The Scholastic distinction is capital. Assuming that the theology of Tillich had some importance, the life of Tillich is no less that of a rather unrespectable man. The latter is independent of the former. Cyril of Alexandria possessed the charism of the doctors all the while being a dubious personage. Reciprocally, Maximilian Kolbe was a witness to Christ but an author of whom it is best to be wary. To return to Husserl and Kierkegaard, their moral rectitude does nothing to persuade us to canonize their contributions to philosophy. And to return to monasticism: let us add therefore that the monk plays the role in late antiquity of the philosopher, and that he wants to be a theologian totally faithful to the definition offered by Evagrius ("One who is a theologian will pray truly.")—but he will almost always be an apprentice, an apprentice philosopher and an apprentice theologian. If saints alone were theologians we could only write the history of theology as a history of "lived theologies." And this history stands out by the shortcomings that it allows . . .

The debate into which we have entered is as old as the spiritual life itself, and whether it be in Christianity or somewhere else, it takes canonical form in the pietist polemic against the *theologia irregenitorum*. Must we have confidence in a professor of theology on account of his science alone, and even on account of a science accompanied by orthodoxy, or must we require of him to have been piously regenerated in the Spirit? In a sense pietism is right to pose this question: if theology is an affair of *theōria* and of *bios*, or if *theōria* ought to include *bios*, we ought not to be satisfied with theological contributions of which

FROM THEOLOGY TO THEOLOGICAL THINKING

we do not know in what contemplation they have their origin. However, pietism is wrong more than right. Ultimately professors are known most often by the traces that they have left—by texts—rather than by a life of which we would have been witnesses, or about which we possess some good witnesses. Texts, after all, can be anonymous or pseudonymous. We know nothing of Pseudo-Dionysius and of the author of the *Macariana*. The necessity of living as a theologian (rightly, or with sanctity) does not cease for all that to weigh on the shoulders of everyone who desires to practice the occupation of theology, and who will then be dedicated to a doing rather than a profession. But we repeat: it is rare to find a theologian who produces good books and offers the witness of a holy life. Edith Stein was a model of rectitude and her works are mediocre. Cyril of Alexandria was a theologian of genius and a troubled person. We admire saints and doctors. But it is as distinct persons that we most often admire them.

Neither philosophy and the philosophical life nor theology and the "theological life" overlap either necessarily or usually. They can overlap: there is no lack of morally respectable philosophers or doctor-saints (the status of "doctor of the Church" was intelligently created). But in the same way that genius can be accompanied by psychological disorder (two examples from the "hardest" sciences spring to mind, Cantor and Gödel), in the same way that it cannot guarantee impeccability, sanctity does not guarantee theoretical excellence. The man devoted to *theoria*, whether philosopher (in the modern sense of the term) or theologian, does not become ipso facto a good theoretician. Reciprocally, the good theoretician may very well be a mediocre "contemplative." The relation between "life" and "work" is most often one of tension. And this requires us to return with prudence to the central place played by *praktike* in both monastic experience and every experience that wants to place itself under its tutelage. *Ascesis* is not the final end of the monk who wants to "attend" to God, to contemplate, to live in the perpetual memory of God, etc. Yet it is also not a step that one day would be completed. The monk is always fasting. The experience of his sin, lived in compunction (in *penthos*) will always accompany him. And if monastic experience is among the experiences that we can classify as eschatological anticipations (and the East and West possess them in abundance; we can be content in mentioning, by way of its artistic trace, Bernini's Teresa of Avila, about which Lacan was surely right to say that he was convinced that she "enjoyed an orgasm" in her ecstasy), then no one, the monk included, is exempt from living in the world and in history. Because he knows himself a sinner, the monk must be judged first on his orthodoxy and then on his orthopraxy. He wants to live the best life possible. He can live it in silence and in peace, *quies hēsukhia*. But his venture will often lead him to speak in order to teach others; and just as teaching enters into view, we necessarily take some distance from the Balthasarian model of a "kneeling theology." The monk's way of life can certainly be called "philosophical" without us being preoccupied with the teaching that he does (supposing that he does more teaching than merely the counsel of an elder to his disciples), for the sole reason that he incarnates a love of wisdom (and not its possession without remainder). In many cases, however, the monk can live his *vita philosophica* without sitting down at a desk to read and write or doing the job of a professor. Further aspects of this story are well known. From very early on, the monk will often be snatched from the monastic life by a bishop who wants to make him a priest. Moreover the monk will often become bishop, and this is still the case in the Christian East, where monks usually receive the episcopate. And even within the walls of the monastery he will often have to play the role of master and scholar—of the *savant, studioso, Wissenschaftler,* briefly, of the one who is not a kneeling theologian, or a theologian only when kneeling. We will return to this in the following lectures. In every case, as a result, *theōria* will not be able to be defined by the sole exercise of contemplation; it will have to be dealt out in concepts and theories and thus with the ever-present risk of being impoverished. And therefore the monk, who appears most

FROM THEOLOGY TO THEOLOGICAL THINKING

often in the history of Christianity (or at least in the *Apoph-thegmata Patrum*) as the uneducated peasant, very quickly dons the vestments of the intellectual. This does not divert him—we hope—from prayer and from *theōria*. However it does tear him away from seclusion or constrains him to interiorize it (Kierkegaard's critique of monasticism loses its force, even its pertinence, when the monk becomes the one who retreats in himself and not in the cloister). There is a strong possibility that this interiorization will be difficult. It is probably easier to attend to God while weaving baskets, and it is probably more difficult to pray while attempting to resolve a theological problem or while writing down the solution that one discovered in a state of prayer. It is not the most insignificant question that theological work can jeopardize the radicality of the monastic project. If we accept the audacity of the words, the monk can cease to be "philosopher" when he becomes a professional theologian. But let us admit that the monk is an animal who shares the *logos*, that the *logos* is not expressed only in the silence of *theōria* or the words of the doxology, and that it is not an aberration or some gloomy destiny that the theology stemming from monasticism (and even while there are still some monks doing theology . . .) often ceases to be a "kneeling theology" in order to take part in the chorus of rational discourses. Ideally, in pagan antiquity the philosopher lives and thinks, and lives what he thinks—and what he "thinks" is both *theōria* and the production of theories. For his part, the monk could not fail initially to form the project of a *theōria* without link to any "intellectual work" whatsoever, but nevertheless would come to see his *theōria* transformed afterward into "theoretical practice." This transition was without doubt very uncomfortable to many, even if this discomfort is rarely admitted. But comfort does not figure among the objects of the monk's desire. Nor, moreover, among the ends of any philosopher faithful to his proper *eros*.

An emphasis ought to be reasserted, at least because in the history of theology it ends by no longer existing or by existing poorly. It is asserted by Evagrius's aphorism that we have already cited. On the one hand, the theologian is the one who prays (to which we must add that prayer was not at all unknown to the pagan philosopher). On the other hand, it is the one who prays *in truth* that merits the title of theologian. The meaning of the double affirmation can be distorted. The theologian, let us say, is the man of *gnōsis*, "if he prays truly," by which we do not mean the practice of a cognitive discipline but a manner of living and knowing—a way of existing. The one who has "partaken of the holy gnosis" (Diadochus of Photice) ipso facto undergoes the experience of prayer: he knows because he prays, or knows in supplicating the "gentleness of God." But in saying this we face a danger, for here we imply the coexistence of two activities, that of the *logos* as *oratio* or *eukhē*, on the one hand, and that of *logos* as intellectual work, on the other. But the danger insinuates itself all the more easily as it is trivially faithful to a division of labor [*sic*] intrinsic to the monastic life. The monk prays and works. In the age of the Fathers of the desert, his work consists in weaving baskets. It can also consist (Evagrius, of the same era, is an example) in writing a treatise on prayer. Recognizing the latter we could forget that the Christian, and the monk a fortiori, are supposed to pray "continually," that they recite the Psalter and weave baskets.

The oldest body of theological writings, the Pauline corpus, provides a path for us. No one has ever doubted that there is a theology of Paul (both an overall Pauline "vision" of the mysteries of Christianity, a Pauline *theōria*, and a stock of theological theses due to Paul). But for our present purpose, let us hasten to recall an obvious fact: the texts in which this theology is spelled out (whether surely Pauline or perhaps deutero-Pauline) is interwoven with prayer and argumentation. Discovering the precise origins of the hymns within Philippians, Ephesians, Colossians, and others (supposing that they are not original creations) is of little interest (here). These hymns, integral parts of the epistles in which they feature, and more than "feature," first—and here is the obvious fact—forbid all disassociation of the didactic and the doxological. If we are asking the Pauline corpus to provide us with a model, prayer is not the preliminary experience "on the knees" of a theological work that is undertaken "seated." The work of theological elaboration is already done in prayer and the writing too. Consequently the motto *ora et labora* ought to be interpreted in another way than is suggested by a naive reading. It does not tell us that the monk and whoever follows his school should pray *then* work, but rather that they ought to pray and work together, in the unity of a single work or *opus Dei*. It is certainly appropriate not to nourish pious illusions. The work of the theologian includes choosing concepts and working with words, rereading sources, comparison of sources, etc., and such work has little chance of being lived as perpetual prayer. The misfortune of the theologian is that his work prevents him out of love for God from always thinking about God while loving him. It is not appropriate, however, to neglect what the monastic texts tell us and, above all, what they invite us to do. They first invite the reader to pray and to learn in a unified way. The privileged example of the chanting of the Psalms is both prayer and a course in theology. They also invite those who follow their school to what we would have to call a doxological practice of writing. Like every other work, it can be done poorly owing to incompetency: the one who prays in truth is certainly a theologian in the existential sense of the term, but no one becomes a theological author because he "knows how" to pray. However, this work can be carried out well, and this is what ought to count here. The unified task of one who prays and writes is a possible task, as is the unified life of the one who does not divide prayer and labor. We will return to this.

TWO

Philosophy, Theology, and the Academy

The transition from late antiquity to the Middle Ages is obscure and remains open to any number of potential periodizations. Intellectual history customarily requires that we propose a name and in this instance the custom is not wrong. We are speaking of Boethius. Boethius matters to the history of philosophy because of his occupation as translator and commentator on Aristotle; he matters to theology because he is the author of important conceptual precisions; and he matters to the history of Christianity because he is a martyr, venerated through the ages under the name of *san Severino*. Briefly, we are interested in his last and most famous work, the *Consolation of Philosophy*. The work is strange, and doubts existed over whether it was written by him for the good reason that nothing about it is explicitly Christian. Under house arrest or in prison, Boethius neither asks for nor receives a divine consolation. Rather, he receives something that seems much different: a consolation carried by philosophy personified. But is the difference so great? The history of the appropriation of philosophical reasons by the Christian *logos* allows us not to believe it. Boethius sets pen to paper after pagan philosophy, or nearly so. In his day *vita philosophica* and *vita christiana* are almost equivalent terms. When asked, about a century before Boethius, about his intellectual identity, Augustine would doubtlessly have responded that he was a Christian philosopher. And if we consider that

Origen's theory of the "spoils of Egypt" was quite common in Christian thought,[1] then we must suspect that the Philosophy that consoles Boethius in his dungeon is a sort of anonymous or pseudonymous Christ. For the "last of the Romans" there is no caesura between what we call "philosophy" and "theology." There is certainly no confusion. Translating Aristotle is one thing and refuting the disciples of Eutyches and Nestorius is another. To pray is one thing and to accept the consolations of philosophy is another. But in both cases, in philosophy as much as theology, speculative competency cannot be disassociated from an existential definition of the philosophical and the theological, which enables the Christian, and the theologian in the most technical sense of the term, to claim without difficulty to be a follower of philosophy and the philosophical life. As we have seen, the monk lives the "philosophical life." The theologian-philosopher Boethius also lives it. And his martyrdom should therefore be understood as an all-encompassing witness to the *logos*, initiator of wisdom, and to the *logos* present in Jesus of Nazareth. Boethius was a practitioner of the concept and of conceptual definition. Let us observe that the definition by which he is commonly known to students, that of the "person," is philosophical as much as theological. And this compels us to say that the one who wants to live life itself, supposing he wants to give himself up to a theoretical work, will then be led to possess a twofold competency, that of the (professional) philosopher and the (professional) theologian. (In a similar way we unproblematically admit that both the moralist philosopher and the philosopher of science are philosophers . . .)

Boethius is an extreme case—at least because we are not absolutely certain that *san Severino*, still honored today in Pavia, is the author of the *Consolation*. And if we must adjudicate about what in his day made for the theological quality of a text, it would doubtless be necessary to tie the adage of Evagrius to the *Confessions* of Augustine. The latter reserves a place for his confessions, for faults committed before his conversion to Christianity. The term "confession," however, is first to be understood in the sense that the book is a vast confession of faith, and even more, a confession of faith developed in such a way that it is concerned with God in the second person, not the third. Augustine confesses his sins and his faith, but not to the reader: he confesses them to a God with whom he is on a first-name basis. Despite the tight conceptuality utilized here and there, the book is above all one very long prayer. And the theology that is elaborated there is certainly the first extra-biblical example available of what we have learned to call a "narrative theology." Augustine tells the story. But he tells it to God. And the confession of one's faith to God is called prayer. Therefore, Augustine is a theologian because he prays in truth. And he prays in truth by placing himself naked *coram Deo.* Here, in the former Milanese rhetorician, theology appears just as it does in his contemporaries, the monks of Scetis or of Lerins: as a mode of life. Independently of his written works, and of its more technical dimensions, the experience of Augustine is that of a man hungry for a certain monasticism. Neither the work accomplished in Cassiciacum among friends, nor later the common life of the bishop of Hippo Regius and his priests, deserves to be taken for a monastic experience. On the other hand, Augustine is an expert—a boffin—who is perpetually engaged in controversies and the resolution of theoretical problems. But whether this is among friends or among bishops and priests (and nothing prohibits the bishop from being friends with his priests . . .), it is clear that theology, in the technical sense of the term, is practiced by Augustine within the horizon of a dream realized in the "rule of Saint Augustine." The person engaged in theoretical work is living. His theoretical work is the fruit of a *theōria.* Here as in monastic experience the leitmotif "ora et labora" is in the foreground: prayer and theoretical work are not two activities but—ideally—a single work with two faces. Pagan philosophers also prayed, or at least composed prayers: thus Cleanthes' hymn to Zeus.[2] Christianity did not radically innovate here. If we would have mentioned the prayer of the philosophers to Augustine or to Anselm of Bec, they would not have been astonished. For the Christian heirs of Socrates, the idea of a philosopher who does not pray would have been the idea of a bad philosopher, incapable of tying together *theōria* and *bios philosophikos.* (This does not exclude the fact that the philosopher can pray to an idol—Zeus—and that the heretics pray to one also: the one who wants to live the philosophical life is not for that reason the holder of correct [religious] opinions.)

Neither Augustine nor Boethius is medieval. But after mentioning the organic unity of "life" and "work" in Augustine, it is necessary to observe forthwith that between antiquity and the Middle Ages until the twelfth century the continuity on this point is seamless. If we wonder what "thinking" means in the Middle Ages, it would be necessary to respond by first drawing attention to their poor knowledge of ancient sources, the accentuated separation of the Latin and Greek worlds, the progressive intervention of the Arab world, etc. These are all important factors, but they do not allow us to identify a rupture and birth of a new age. In antiquity, philosophy and theology are ways of life as much as they are discourses and modes of knowledge. These ways of life are tied to specific organizations of work and life. It is true that this work has its products in written works. But can we measure it by these written works alone? Absolutely not. In antiquity the philosopher and theologian are first defined as those who live a philosophical or theological life. For a number of centuries after Boethius, in the Latin world no one will step up any longer to live as a philosopher. These centuries belonged to theology, or in any case to a discourse that is ignorant of any strict division between theology and philosophy. This affiliation finally had its concrete logics. Theology had its places to be lived and to be produced. Regarding theological theories, diversity evidently reigned. The opposition of theories, however, comes about after the unity of *theōria.* And if this unity reigned, it always reigns, therefore, in the places of work and starting from them. One must look at these places in order to ask whether and how a new epoch was born.

(a) Until the twelfth century, theology and philosophy in the

Latin world (to which we will restrain our attention) are not developed in a single place. They are developed in monastic schools. They are also developed in cathedral schools and canonical schools. In all three cases, we have spoken of "schools." The term and the phenomenon are evidently not new. Both Plato and Aristotle founded schools. Distinguished theological and exegetical schools existed in Alexandria and Antioch. To found a school is the destiny, not always enviable, of every great thinker. It is therefore not surprising to discover the schools of Chartres or Laon. And above all it is not surprising that these schools are distinguished less by means of a conceptual patrimony or by a specific theory (even if they possessed patrimonies) than by their association, as we have said, with a specific *eros:* of a *theōria* that embraces (spiritual) life and intellectual work. The motto "ora et labora" clearly holds good for the monastic schools but also for all the communities of work and teaching founded outside the monastic movement.

What are we concerned with now? To state it simply: with the link between intellectual work and its place. To be Platonic or Aristotelian in late antiquity, there was evidently no need to live in Athens, nor to belong to some Platonic or Aristotelian fraternity. A certain theoretical agreement was enough. Yet to speak first of theoretical agreement in order to define the medieval schools would be inaccurate. (Just as it would be horribly inaccurate to speak of theoretical agreement in order to define the ambition of the first monastic communities of Egypt and Palestine.) A school often possesses its own theoretical traditions. However, it possesses them secondarily. And what it possesses in the first place is a way of life common to masters and students. The monastic school, of Bec for example, is a school within a monastery, and its students are first monks, then students. They are students of theology (if we can accept giving them this slightly anachronistic title) who follow a prescribed course, certainly, but they first belong to a community for which scholarly work is not the privileged end: the students work collectively to understand what they believe only by being engaged together in the *opus Dei*. To put it another way: the intellectual work with which they are engaged is an integral part of the *opus Dei*. This work is always carried out somewhere—in such or such abbey, or such or such canonical community, in the shadow of such or such cathedral, all of which possess their own intellectual tradition, eminent or not. All intellectual work (and all work whatsoever) clearly must be carried out somewhere; all work participates in a tradition, remarkable or not. Our point here could pass for a platitude. However, it is not one. The circulation of manuscripts, the wandering of students from one school to another—all this makes intellectual work, in the Middle Ages like any other time, an almost nomadic work. To work "here" or "there" does not necessarily designate membership in a place of teaching or of research [*sic*]. But the history of the schools known to us reveals their remarkable resistance to this process of nonmembership. Wherever he goes the student meets new masters, but the places of teaching are ruled by the same principles. The same proposal is made: that of the "theoretical life." And where it is made, this proposal is simultaneously that of a knowledge (delivered under the form of theories) and that of the participation in the life of a community of which the first end is to attend to God and only then to speak well about him (or about that which is not God: the school is not only a school of theology). Clearly it is easy to single out some tendencies that draw together diverse places of teaching. However, the bonds between way of life and way of thought can be tied differently at different places. Finally, the schools have a history punctuated by the influence of a renowned scholar who is succeeded by others: hence the school at Bec, where the prestige of Lanfranc attracted Anselm, but to which Anselm gave new impulses. Each school, therefore, has its own inflections. Anselm's thought ties doxology and speculation, the Cistercian masters are kerygmatic and doxological more than conceptual, the masters of Saint Victor are both didactic and speculative. These are all distinctions that need refining, and which are indeed refined over the generations. But however we distinguish them, the unity that reigns in all these places among diverse ways of living and thinking is clearly greater than every difference. The school of theology in whatever place is in a united way a place of intellectual work and a place of theological life. The school does not teach only theology (in fact, it teaches almost every available knowledge of its day), but theology, which does not yet possess its technical name, is not a discipline among disciplines. It is not even the queen of the disciplines. Just like early monastic experience, it is a form of life. If theology exists, it certainly arises from a *theōria*, or is bathed in it. Here again, *theōria* is indissociable from a practice. The contours or definition of such practice are without doubt vaster than that of Evagrian *praktikē*. But both are tied together: what the school proposes is training in the Christian life, indissociable from a theoretical work and giving this work its exact sense.

(b) To be more precise, this work is (the twelfth century included) practiced independently of every philosophy endowed with an independence. Paganism is certainly not dead in the West (but the fight against paganism is no longer anything but a rearguard combat conducted in the countryside). In any case, pagan philosophy has disappeared. The Christian thinkers of this era are somewhat familiar with Judaism, some know a little Islam—in the first half of the twelfth century Peter the Venerable translates the Koran into Latin—and they know them as living and imminent realities. Pagan philosophy is from now on absent from the scene. Some Greek and Latin philosophical texts have survived the shipwreck of classical culture. However, no one speaking as a philosopher is present in the monastic, canonical, or cathedral schools. One will certainly examine the identity of John Scotus Erigena, among the most "philosophical" of thinkers of these centuries—though as a thinker of the uncreated and created, he could not conceive of himself as a philosopher, or could only be ignorant of the distinction of the philosophical and theological or, if he philosophized, do it in service to a project that is completely theological. The classical philosopher seemed unlike the Christian when he accused the Christian of sinning against both the *logos* and common sense; and Christianity, in its various places, reciprocally considered philosophy as unlike itself, to the point of considering the Greek *logos* to be a sick *logos* (thus Theodoret in his *Therapy*). On the contrary, in the time of Anselm, Yves of Chartres, or Gilbert of Poitiers there is no philosopher present to pose objections to Christianity, and antiphilosophism, exemplarily that of Bernard of Clairvaux, does not include a hostility toward the pagan economy of knowledge but a polemic against theologies deemed theologically evil (in his case, that of Abelard). Erigena is clearly nourished by Platonism. The lessons that Augustine received from the *libri platonici* are present in the Chartreans and Victorines. The medieval Christian reception of classical philosophy occurs in two ways: by the medievals' philosophical and theological readings. There is a reception of pagan philosophy, but in the absence of any thinker whatsoever who is defined as philosopher and only as philosopher. Neither Augustine nor Boethius knew of such a situation. It is the index of a new time.

(c) What we just said could be said more dramatically. We would be just as right to speak of a concentration of (nearly) all knowledge into the hands of the one whose mission is to speak of God, the God of Jesus Christ. To speak of knowledge, here, is to speak of encyclopedic knowledge (which is also the case for medieval Judaism or Islam). It is about some skills that the theologian does not have to master in order to be a theologian: for example, the theologian often does not very well need to be a doctor. On the other hand, it is about some kinds of knowledge that it would be necessary to possess in order to speak better about God but which in themselves tell us nothing about him: grammar, rhetoric, and dialectic are not theological disciplines. However, these are, in a totally positive sense, pre-theological disciplines: prerequisites to a theology worthy of the schools where it is elaborated and taught. The totality of knowledge— knowledge that pretends to the universal—is handed over to the one whose business it is to speak of God. It is necessary here to take the measure of the phenomenon and, above all, not be spellbound by it. Encyclopedism is only real in the Middle Ages because it is possible. The books to be read are few in number, and consequently the scholar can easily be a universal scholar—which is a possibility up to Leibniz, after whom no one can be a scholar but in a regional way. A postmedieval case merits being recalled here. Bellarmine was opposed to the astronomy of Galileo and it is easy to accuse him of obscurantism and ignorance. The truth, however, is found somewhere else. Bellarmine's knowledge of astronomy was near that of Galileo, for the good reason that any scholar in the time of Bellarmine and Galileo knows all the astronomy there is to know—that is to say, of course, only a little astronomy. Bellarmine was opposed to Galileo just as any "normal" science is opposed to "revolutionary" science. Bellarmine certainly had some theological reasons to support his opposition and these reasons were erroneous. In any case, the conflict did not oppose theology and science. It opposed, as paradoxically as it seems, a scientist of genius to a scientist incapable of accepting a theoretical revolution (a revolution, further, that Galileo proposed as not provoking any theological difficulty . . .). In order to interpret these centuries, then, it is fitting a fortiori to perceive clearly that something other than theological knowledge is known (grammar, dialectic, etc.), but that nothing that is known is unknown to the theologian. We would be at pains, reciprocally, to identify a Christian intellectual who does not possess theological competence. Bernard and Abelard—another classic polemic—do not share the same theoretical interests or the same theological method (they differ here beyond recognition), but they share a culture, varying in each according to the places that they acquired it, but in variations that do not condemn them to a dialogue of the deaf. With the scholar seeking (nearly) all knowledge, the student was consequently devoted to all the knowledge of the day. And so long as this knowledge [*savoir*] was not acquired in a heteroclite manner, as a simple accumulation of specific kinds of knowledge [*connaissances*], then a unified totalization was possible. The idea of specialization is therefore to be handled with prudence when one speaks of schools where everyone learned everything. The theologian could not appear as a specialist in an organization of knowledge where he is not constrained merely to know theology. Until the twelfth century, every place of learning dispenses a little theology to everyone. And be that as it may, certainly no one teaches there who does not possess true theological competence.

To speak of a school is to speak of scholars, and it could easily be concluded that the centuries we have been looking at were dedicated to making coexist two conceptions of the theological, a conception of the theological "life" and of the theologian's "occupation." As in the patristic era, these two notions coexisted without danger: theology can be content being lived; it can be taught as much as lived; and we cannot disassociate either aspect from its practice. (But we ought to recognize the duality of this practice . . .) Confrontations certainly took place and we have already mentioned one. A theology born of contemplation (of a *theōria* that does not necessarily aim to produce theories), like that of Bernard of Clairvaux, could not accept the dialectical exercises of Abelard. A theology predetermined toward prayer evidently could not accommodate a work whose concept gives every appearance of sparing no place at all for the exigencies of the spiritual life. We are certainly called to circumspection here. We know these confrontations only through the mediation of the textual traces they have left; the tension of which we speak, theology as *opus Dei* and as occupation, was inevitably lived by every thinker of the epoch as an essential trait of the theological; causes célèbres are always rare, but that which shines in them here was necessarily the daily bread of the theological life of the epoch. In any case the school—first as place of teaching, then as place of the production of knowledge, finally as place of the transmission of what was elaborated there in an original way—is the dominating institution of the epoch. The notion of "institution" must be taken back up again. No statute is necessarily involved. The monastery includes *studium* and students, but the sole rule that governs it is that of Saint Benedict, to which local customs are added. The canonical school is hardly more instituted: each community of canons regular, here again, chooses its modalities of teaching—being understood that, in the case of the canonical school as well as the monastic school, the communities are always set within networks of communities, masters often pass from one place to another, the reputation of a *studium* often draws novices from afar, and being well understood, therefore, that in relation to a multitude of schools we can legitimately say that they follow a "model." And if the cathedral school truly merits being called "instituted" (purely and simply being created out of nothing and endowed with statutes from its very beginning), it will vary all the while depending on whether it wants to be only a dispenser of knowledge or a depository of all the different kinds of knowledge of its time—and therefore the designated shelter for the best minds of a diocese or for more than a diocese. This does not mean that anarchy reigned. In the Middle Ages the order of studies is almost immutably fixed, from the *trivium* to theological studies. Not only do programs of study exist, but they are in operation everywhere. But this means, and the point is decisive for us, that the relation of master and disciple takes on a new face. Already in classical antiquity the master could don the garments of the professor. We possess some of Aristotle's courses. From the beginning of the second century, Christianity possesses some places of professorial teaching: the catechetical school of Alexandria was no doubt the first. And therefore in the Middle Ages the practical organization of the schools means that the master appears to us first as professor.

Yet it is also a key point that the master is certainly not reduced to this role. The professor teaches, and he also writes; what he writes flows from what he teaches: the greatest merit of Karl Barth, as historian of theology, was to prove that Anselm was not a theologian and a philosopher mashed together, and that his apparently most metaphysical texts (but what does "metaphysical" actually mean here?) can be understood only as they give themselves to be understood, as a prayer. Here and elsewhere (without doubt Cistercian theology furnishes us with the best example) instruction [*didascalie*] and doxology are taken as a whole or refused as a whole. The proof of this is found in the local unity of the church and classroom.

Grammar, rhetoric, and dialectic are certainly tools for theology, but they are still not theological disciplines. However, until the emergence of the university, the school guarantees to them the status of auxiliaries of theology. (One should not complain about it: the mastery of language inevitably enters into theological work.) It enters into every liturgical formula straight out of rhetoric. Judging by the literature consecrated to "Anselm's proof," the logical framework of the *Monologion* is still today worth being taken into consideration,[3] and the author of the *Monologion* was a professor before becoming bishop. The schools, whether monastic, canonical, or cathedral, were not schools of theology and only theology—so much so that one can legitimately wonder, truth be told, whether a school that was theological and only theological would be possible . . . This is the major point: the schools were nothing less than places of theological experience, and at their summit, places of the experience of God in prayer. But it is this which is going to disappear with the arrival of the new place called the University. Its appearance is well known and it is sufficient to recall some of the major facts. (a) The first is the radicalization, as a self-conscious project, of that which has formerly never been clearly intended, the coexistence under the same roof of the totality of knowledge. *Universitas scientiarum* signifies an inclusion and an exclusion. An inclusion in the sense that no *scientia* (we should speak of "knowledge" here, since science does not truly exist yet) is absent from the University: everything that merits being known at the end of an intellectual work is offered there to the student. The exclusion is found in the fact that whatever is not taught in the University is ipso facto deprived of the dignity of knowledge (of "science"). The arts, in the modern sense of the term, are not taught in the University. The technical arts, handicrafts (the art of which is assimilated to the former), are not taught there either. And if it is easy to admit that embroidery is not a university discipline (however, the situation will be modified somewhat on the far-off day when the history of art becomes a university discipline alongside every other kind of history, including the history of the university institution), one senses in any case that the University is defined by its power to make long-range decisions about the topology of knowledge. To speak of the totality of knowledge is to speak of the totality of knowledge recognized as such. And the one who maintains this discourse is also given the power to circumscribe the various kinds of knowledge: the University is only a federation of faculties, but nevertheless a topology of knowledge is available, by way of evidence or decree, which allows it to institute the faculties. (b) The second fact is philosophy's return on the scene or, perhaps, its first entrance as independent knowledge. The arrival in the Latin world of the Philosopher, flanked by his Commentator, had two consequences: it reorganized the intellectual scene of Christianity while organizing the University's distribution of tasks, entitlements, and duties. Christianity, whether it presented itself as a non-philosophy or as the true philosophy, has never been unaware of the existence of philosophy. Medieval, pre-university Christianity was not unaware of it either, despite the scarcity of available sources. For a long time Anselm was understood as a theologian and "metaphysician" (and the latter in a distinct way from the former). But in the time of Anselm or Gilbert of Poitiers, the distinction did not truly exist, and it did not exist before them either. Augustine made a major contribution to the theory of time in the middle of a work composed as both a theological autobiography and a prayer. For Justin of Nablus before him, access to Christianity was made at the end of a journey where he had visited the dominant philosophies of his time, and his conversion was made with as much continuity as discontinuity. And in the schools of the pre-university period, philosophy existed neither as prolegomena to theology nor as its parallel discipline: the univocal concepts of philosophy and theology are missing, every strict separation is absent and, inevitably, every precise distribution of tasks likewise. But when a new philosophy comes on the scene in the Latin world, its appearance coincides with the foundation of the institutional place where it will be taught, and it will be taught at a distance from theology. By means of its insertion into the University, for the first time in history philosophy possesses a real autonomy, on the one hand, and it becomes a reality recognized within the Christian organization of kinds of knowledge, on the other. The Philosopher is clearly not the first philosopher that the Christian West had known. But Latin Aristotelianism, lodged in a university department all to itself (the "faculty" of philosophy), is probably the first philosophy to have been treated in the Christian milieu as authorized to exercise a theological influence all the while absolutely not being theology—and it is no exaggeration to say that we owe to it a disassociation of the theological and philosophical which never existed before. Theology, however, is no longer a philosophy, and we can speak of it without hesitating over the terms, even if the commencing University does not yet speak of "theology" in our terms.[4] Theology holds a place that pertains to it exclusively—even its own "faculty" (while the Philosopher possesses his own). And during the first decades of the university experience, it possesses a faculty consecrated almost exclusively to the transmission of its thinking. As a result it is no marvel that theology becomes a titular discipline of a well-delimited domain. The consequence is inevitable: the fragmentation of knowledge. Of course, knowledge in the schools was parceled out: grammar was not "sacred doctrine" and no one doubted this. This fragmentation, however, did not really touch the block constituted by philosophy and theology; and it is this block, this nearly unified domain, that is broken into two fragments when the University is constituted. In the medieval University the faculty of philosophy taught only philosophy. (It therefore becomes possible to devote oneself to philosophy alone.) Even if the theologian has the right to intervene in philosophical matters, he himself teaches only theology (the most philosophical of the "disputed questions" of Thomas Aquinas have a theological finality, and his commentaries on Aristotle are not the fruit of teaching but of a research parallel to his work as "master of the sacred page"). The statutes of the university are evidently made to guarantee a complementarity. Philosophical work is one thing, and theological work another, but if the university project is realized, the two come up against no contradiction; and a theologian, Thomas, will be found in his day to be the best commentator on Aristotle—much better than a master of arts seeking to Christianize Aristotle's thought, which was not Aquinas's intention. Hence, and it is precisely here that a new epoch commences, the dialogue between a Greek and Christian *logos* in the same thinker is substituted in the University for an institutionally governed dialogue between representatives of two specialties. Now a Latin word, *scientia*, deserves to replace *logos*. *Logos*, "logic," the link between rationality and words—there is clearly nothing here that the theologian and philosopher of the university had to disown. Yet *scientia* (which is not yet science but will end up becoming it) indicates a desire for rigorous knowledge that is perfectly Greek. Hence, in the University, each is an official representative of a different "science." And if the privilege of the theologian is to practice a "sacred" doctrine, while philosophy is a profane discipline, his practice is still limited: he only practices "*sacra doctrina*," which ought to suffice for him, but which will necessarily stir up trouble through its relationship with the philosopher. Conceptual couples—order of nature, order of grace; profane doctrine, sacred doctrine, etc.—will not be lacking in the subsequent history of theology in order to justify the division of work instituted by the medieval University. Even so, it is not certain that these conceptual distinctions concealed what is precarious in this division. (c) If we finally ask the theologian to take a position in relation to the Philosopher and to every philosophy, the position will be unambiguous: philosophy exists in order to furnish the theologian with new concepts. The most well known case, which deserves to be such, is the fascination exercised on university theology by the Aristotelian theory of causality.[5] Whoever does not invoke this theory in the thirteenth century does not deserve to don the vestments of the university theologian. It is the case in the future "Common Doctor" of course, and it is also the case in Bonaventure: as un-Aristotelian as possible, he no less feels the obligation to give his commentary on the *Sentences* a prologue in the form of a promise: the subject will be treated faithfully to the Aristotelian schema. Other Aristotelian theories will enter into the *organon* of the theologian. A little awkwardly, hylomorphism provides its conceptual structure for Thomas's theory of the sacraments, and in the same way it governs his theory of the relation of soul and body. The philosophical ethics of virtues (a term that only appeared three times in the New Testament, and each time with virtually no conceptual charge) provides the base for the majority of moral theories taught in the faculties of theology. And if it happens that a theological topic cannot be treated with the "weapons of Aristotle" (Maritain), the theologian will only have two solutions at his disposal, either more or less to ignore this topic or else treat it without philosophical reference: it is in this way that history is under-thought in Thomas Aquinas whereas in Bonaventure it enjoys an ample treatment that is almost exclusively biblical. Scholastic theology has been accused of being abstract, but it is more simply a theology that practices with enthusiasm, and sometimes without discernment, the theory of the "spoils of the Egyptians" proposed a millennium earlier. (Of course, it was not the first theology to put this theory into practice . . .)

The enthusiasm could be intemperate, but numerous masters of theology possessed real philosophical competence: the university division of labor could have been practiced smoothly, in anticipation of a theory of "frontier questions" that is a bit more astute. Discord, however, was not lacking. From the Parisian condemnations of 1277, followed by Kilwardby's condemnations in Oxford, two phenomena are evident. The first is that the theologians could be left naively fascinated by philosophical fashions—among the condemned propositions only a few, incidentally, are of Thomist origin. The second and without doubt more important is that the philosophers, whom the rules of the University prohibit from encroaching on the terrain of the theologians, eventually no longer maintain an autonomous philosophical discourse by disassociating their own rationality from theological reason and end up contradicting the discourse of the theologian and sometimes contradicting the common teaching of Christianity. Institutionally defined as a non-theologian, the philosopher inevitably understood himself as such—and universities did not exist long before this happened. More dramatically, the philosopher will end up understanding himself *only* as a philosopher. Non-theologian certainly does not mean non-Christian. But in the philosophers condemned in Paris and Oxford, in the propositions condemned and in the rest of their work, we often see a certain bracketing of the Christian identity. The bracketing was theoretically necessary, since the members of the faculty of arts had no other right than to be philosophers, and they played this card abundantly. A new kind of practice also came on the scene, for along with the appearance of a philosophical work closed in on itself also came the idea of a "philosophical life" distinct from the "theological life." As practiced by the brilliant masters of arts in Paris, philosophy is a game without religious reference. The territory of the philosopher is certainly assigned by a foundational authority, secular and religious, which recognizes both a right to philosophy and a duty of the philosopher. The concession of a territory could nevertheless be shown to be insufficient. As long as the philosopher passionately wants to be a philosopher he cannot help investing his work with vital significance. In the last instance he can only desire to live a *vita philosophica*, or teach what this would be. For the one who conceives of the philosophical life in the school of Aristotle, the highest virtue will be magnanimity. But short of considerable qualifications, is an ethics of magnanimity tenable on Christian terrain? The answer goes without saying. And if the philosopher tries to ensure to magnanimity the highest role, not only as an exegete of Aristotle but also in his own name, he will inevitably come to suggest that "Humility is not a virtue";[6]

and he will inevitably be censured by an ecclesiastical authority that, in the preceding centuries, had not shied away from condemnations, but had also never had to confront the problem of an emancipated philosophical discourse. We ought not to confuse the trial of Abelard with the condemnations of Siger or Boethius of Dacia: the situation to which the experts of Etienne Tempier respond in 1277 is totally new.

To occupy the role of philosopher in the university does not inevitably lead to being only a philosopher and to living only a "philosophical life." The fragmentation of knowledge at the heart of the University is in any case a major fact, one that signifies the end of a long era—the era when the "Christian life" and the "philosophical life" were more or less equivalent. In the middle of the thirteenth century, Paris is witness to a particularly significant event: the erection, a stone's throw away from the university, of a Cistercian convent ("Bernardine") destined to allow young religious to be initiated into a new theology developed outside of all monastic influence. From now on theology is a "science," *scientia*. Thomas Aquinas surely understands by "science" what we call "knowledge." If theology is a "science" it is on the (Aristotelian!) model of "subaltern sciences," of kinds of knowledge that take their principles from other kinds of knowledge: just as music borrows its principles from mathematics, so our historical knowledge of God is subaltern to the knowledge of God by the angels and the blessed (to whom we clearly do not attribute a "science" of God in the modern sense of the term . . .). Monastic theology and the theologies like it never pretended to a "scientific" status completely unknown to them. They were satisfied with maintaining a rigorous language and claiming to be adherents of *theōria* or *consideratio*. But in the time of academic theology, monastic theology (and theologies like it) are condemned to death by the fascination exercised by the Philosopher and by the theology that accepted his influence, and they condemn themselves to death by becoming followers of the School. And much later, it is indeed remarkable that the movement to refound monasticism in the nineteenth century totally ignored the theological tradition proper to monasticism. The refounded monasticism was intellectually modern: mainly influenced by the Neo-Scholastic movement. This was without doubt the spirit of the times. Did it not also appear in the fact that theology, in the time of Dom Guéranger, appeared to have acquired its definitive stature only in the context of the medieval University?

To teach is to teach: to transmit knowledge. There are, however, different ways to teach. And if at the end of the twelfth century theology is provided with a new place of teaching, we must also add that this provision is accompanied by the birth of a new tool for teaching, the "question," *quaestio*. The tool had to affect the content. With the practice of the "question," within the commentaries of the *Sentences*, in the "disputed" questions or "quodlibets," the confrontation and evaluation of theories did not make *theōria* disappear—it relegated it, if you like, to the background or to the level of the preliminary. The "question" was an instrument of powerful work, which doubtless explains its success (another factor is certainly its ease of use). This instrument of work also mobilized a totally prosaic language that was almost ready-made for formalization (Thomas Aquinas composed poetry but nothing from his poetic streak shines through in his teaching).[7] This could have or should have led pre-Scholastic theology, monastic theology above all, to refuse being cast in the molds of the new norms. This was not the case. And whereas, in the monastic milieu, theology ordinarily attempted to model its language on the language of the scriptures upon which it commented, here the language and scriptural commentary are no longer present, for the one who comments on the *Sentences* or engages in a similar exercise does so under the form provided by the authorities that are invoked. (We can also add that the scriptural commentaries of Thomas Aquinas, an important figure in this exercise, are written in a completely different language from that of the commented-upon texts . . .) The commentary on the *Sentences* is certainly not the first word of university theology, and it occurs only after a course in biblical studies—yet it is in view of the commentary on the *Sentences* and in order to prepare for its logic that one comments on the scriptures: one becomes a biblical bachelor only in order then to become a bachelor of the *Sentences*. So, a new place for theological teaching, a new division of tasks, and finally, a new language: the continuity of the faith confessed (and, one hopes, lived) cannot mask the interruption.

Among other things, medieval Aristotelianism lived out a passion for novelty. The appearance of the *quaestio* and the style of writing particular to the School will equally sustain a fascination. The apologists of Neo-Scholastic theology in the twentieth century did not hide their disdain for pre-Scholastic theology.[8] They understood, at least, what university theology introduced: an almost naive taste for progress. This appetite was a new phenomenon. We would have to take great pains to identify a real discontinuity, other than of detail, between the form and content of the theology of the Pauline epistles and that of Bernard of Clairvaux. Assuredly, there was no lack of debates. The debates never ceased about the proper way to interpret scripture. But whatever they were, these debates among diverse versions of correct opinion or among right and wrong opinions, had always been formulated in the same style of theological writing. The patristic era sometimes exhibited a discourse as dry as it was abundantly conceptual, so much so that the temptation emerges to speak of a pre-Scholasticism—for example, in the *Corpus Leontianum*. The university *quaestio* is not without a past—the *Questions to Thalassius* of Maximus the Confessor should figure in its genealogy. But despite the polemics and the concentrated work on the concept, the master always ended up donning the vestments of the mystagogue. In university theology, however, mystagogy disappears for the sake of a conceptualization of the mystery. Bonaventure, of course, stands out as an exception. This conceptualization does not compare to Hegelian absolute knowledge. The two are probably not related. The fact remains that the Scholastic sliding from an introduction to the mystery to the conceptualization of the mystery is not a mere detail in the history of theology . . .

We have spoken of the Philosopher, whose work eclipses every other philosophy (but were other philosophers known during the short absolute reign of Aristotelianism?). A dissymmetry ought then to be noted: university theology, up to the end of the Middle Ages, is never endowed with a Theologian (a "common doctor") whose authority is admitted by everyone. The authority of the Philosopher was uncontested only for a very brief time. And theology always lived its university unity in the mode of a plurality. The schools that made up the School always kept the same mode of research and the same style of expression. In any case, they did it without ever a doctor being imposed on them as the Doctor par excellence and without his doctrine being imposed as the theology of reference. Here again, the Neo-Scholastic (i.e., Neo-Thomist) historiographies tell us the truth in their very act of concealing it. Taking the opposite view to theirs is the best way to understand the dispersion of the faculty of theology in the schools, a dispersion, no less, that was tolerated without any theoretical difficulty, no school having the means to impose itself as exemplary representative of the School (that there were institutional difficulties, as was also the case in the faculty of philosophy, is another problem). Aristotle was the great master of the Scholastics, however briefly, but no theologian ever passed as the Master par excellence. And if more than one doctor had a posterity, and if his disciples often sought to assume power in the faculty of theology, we should at least meditate on the case of Bonaventure, who had the good luck of not having disciples—there were no Bonaventurians—and of not "founding a school." The plurality of schools in the faculty of theology is a given from the beginning of the University. In the eighteenth century, Benedict XIV will pour forth encouragements to a phenomenon present since the thirteenth century . . .[9]

In any case, regarding the coexistence of the faculties of philosophy and theology, one thing is clear after the episode of 1277: the foundation of the universities proceeded from a project that was a great dream, that of the harmonious transmission (and production) of every kind of knowledge, yet the situation reigning two generations later was that of a "conflict of faculties." There is certainly no lack of works that claim to realize the success of the university program: the *Summa contra gentiles* is the accomplished model of a discourse that is first purely philosophical and then purely theological without rupture or internal contradiction. Yet here we are dealing with a brilliant exception. The self-understanding of medieval theology can be articulated in the scholarly formula "philosophia ancilla theologiae." But the philosopher never accepted the rule they tried to impose on him (unless he was also a theologian). The *De primo principio* of Duns Scotus, the "ways" to God in the *Summa theologiae* and other texts, come to us from authors who combined theological creativity with philosophical creativity. But among the majority of professional philosophers (and neither Thomas nor Duns Scotus practiced the profession of philosopher), to be a philosopher is to be only a philosopher and a philosopher vowed to express no interest in theology. His discourse is a closed discourse because it is elaborated in a closed field. This discourse only serves theology to the degree that the theologian decides to be served by it—we never encounter philosophical texts that expressly claim to be auxiliaries to theology. The philosophy of religion does not yet exist. The philosophy of revelation even less so. The philosopher is not authorized to encroach on the terrain of the theologian. A distancing was therefore inevitable. University philosophy, whether envisaged as a profession or way or mode of life, is necessarily indifferent to theology (and bears no responsibility toward it). What is more unsettling is that it never indicates its limits, which it could only do by receiving a theological point of view on itself: the auditor of Siger or of Boethius of Dacia is perhaps interested in theology, and he will perhaps begin studies in theology after receiving his diploma in philosophy, but nothing within the teaching provided by the members of the faculty of arts leads to theology.[10] Philosophically speaking, the latter is another "science," more other than the mathematics of the twentieth century are other to the biology of the same century. The epoch certainly sees a triumph of theology despite the censure of some theological theses. The masters of arts at the University of Paris carry less weight than the masters of theology. And the reason why we are interested so much in the members of the faculty of arts is not mysterious: it is what we live in the twenty-first century, a time when philosophy is more interesting than theology and when there is no lack of specialists who wish that the medieval philosophers were more interesting than the theologians who were their neighbors. But the judgment of Gilson is always valuable: however important medieval philosophy may be, it is erroneous to imagine a Middle Ages crowded with philosophers while it was first crowded with theologians, whatever the real importance of medieval philosophy. Let us only add to Gilson by saying that the Middle Ages is crowded with theologians but the philosopher is never far away, and their encounter, if by chance there be one, will always be an event with an uncertain outcome.

In any case it must be conceded that what we see emerge with the university division of knowledge is, however we interpret it, nothing other than modernity, or its first moments. In the Latin world philosophy finally comes to appear as something other than theology. Theology comes to appear as something other than philosophy. Life according to philosophy and life according to theology are from now on two. The new times would have seemed strange to Erigena or Gilbert of Poitiers. And if we try to identify a caesura between one world and the other, it is useless to search anywhere else but in the epistemic revolution of which the University was the place and principal cause.

We have spoken of the conflict of faculties. The expression is not medieval but Kantian, forged at a time when "scientia" had disappeared to the profit of science, in the sense that we understand the term today. The transition had a theoretical face and a practical face. Science appeared under the form that it still retains in the projects and labors of Galileo. Let us remember that it had as its origin and end the mathematization of the whole of being. Bacon furnishes a complementary theory. And let us remember here that science is designated as end and means of submitting nature to the question, that experimentation forces the real to admit what it is. The new world superimposed on the lifeworld,[11] as well as the new practice of the acquisition of knowledge, together could not do anything but rebound, if not onto theology (the epistemology of Bacon purely and simply puts it to death whereas that of Galileo puts it in brackets), at least onto the place that it occupied in the University. The theologians were certainly not intimidated before the experimentalism that imposed itself at the end of the sixteenth century. Some great thinkers carried their share of theology and proved the noncontradiction of the worlds of faith and science: Descartes, Pascal, Leibniz. As for university theology, it imperturbably pursued its work: Bacon and Galileo did not interfere with Baroque Scholasticism (and, even more, Baroque Scholasticism did not toil fruitlessly). The fact remains that at the very moment that theology suffers the attacks of what would become the Enlightenment, and then the attacks of the Enlightenment full stop, its position in the University becomes progressively more unstable. The fact of this instability does not mean that science chased theology from the University. Yet in light of this fact we must acknowledge that theology is incontestably a "scientia" but is not a science: a rigorous work is not for that reason a scientific work. There will still be, and there still are, places of teaching adorned with the title of university where theology is the "queen of the sciences": paradigmatically the universities called "pontifical," universities that have never claimed to accommodate the *universitas scientiarum* and where only philosophy and canon law are present besides theology (and sometimes a little more). The definition of theology as "science," traceable back to the seventeenth century, was ritually repeated by the late representatives of the School (thus in the Carmelites of Salamanca). But at the very moment that Leibniz formulates the project of a totally scientific philosophy (a project certainly formed outside the university), it is virtually self-evident to everyone that theology must be redefined or perish. History tells us that it knew how to redefine itself.

First, however, a flashback is necessary. Galileo and Bacon did not have a theological care at all, but they appear after a violent reaction against the theology (and philosophy) of the School. This reaction is tied to the person of Luther. There is no lack of information about the reasons that pushed Dr. Martin to refuse to play the Scholastic game. He learned theology under its nominalist version, and nominalist theology sins through an evident aridity (the fact that nominalism weighed heavily in his theology is another matter). In the era of Gabriel Biel, however, nominalist theology stands among the medieval theologies for which the philosophical points of view are the most alive. But when Luther writes his *Disputatio contra theologiam scholasticam*, the viciously anti-Aristotelian accent can hide neither that Aristotle is not the sole target nor that the author of the theses takes as his adversary any theology that requires any Philosopher whatsoever. As envisaged by Luther, theology is evidently not a science and is not even a "scientia"—it can only go under the name of a "practical science." This makes us regret that Luther had not crossed Bonaventure and Scotus on his path. And as envisaged by Luther, therefore, theology takes the greatest distance possible from all philosophy. Luther's philosophical influences are evident, but it is also evident that he conceives theology as non-philosophy.[12] Biblical commentary again becomes the theological exercise par excellence and preaching again becomes a place for the elaboration of theological discourse. (This was the case in Augustine and almost all the pre-Scholastic fathers and doctors, but Eckhart was the sole thinker of the School for whom preaching had been more than a work of popularization—the only one to think while preaching.) Theology is therefore only theology. There is nothing new here: the universities already defined theology in this way. However, Luther's protest (if theology is only theology, Aristotle cannot teach the theologian anything) did not merely perform a work of delimitation, and a violent one, which he only did by refusing the academic organization of knowledge. He did more: he denied in advance that the epistemologies of Bacon and Galileo had any theological import. But he therefore failed to take up a position in relation to them. Theology, as Luther conceived it, is immunized in advance from any critique that the science going to be born could raise against it—there could be no conflict for the good reason that there was not, or ought not to be, any border between them. Immunization was merit-worthy in theory (in theological theory and in it alone); and the Lutheran withdrawal of theology into itself prevented theology neither from continuing, after Luther, to participate in the labors of the University nor, above all, from encountering greater and greater difficulties in this participation. Luther left the University, and neither Calvin, nor Zwingli, nor Bucer took part in university tasks, although the destiny of Protestant theology since Melanchthon and Ramus was to continue to take its seat at the table of academic disciplines (how could a secession have been truly possible?) in order finally to be compelled to argue that it had the right to be included. Its available choices were to redefine its position in the context of the University and by relation to the faculty of theology, to defend its place among the university disciplines, or, of course, to perpetuate the medieval university structure. The seventeenth century saw Lutheran theology structure itself as a scholastic neighbor to a faculty of philosophy that placed no interdict on theology—in many respects, Lutheran Scholasticism knew how to avoid any conflict of the faculties. The eighteenth century saw Protestant theology almost hopelessly attempt to come to terms with the scientific culture and criticisms of the Enlightenment. Finally, in the same period, Catholic theology took two directions: either the strict maintenance of the medieval organization of studies in universities that kept a prudent distance from the active theological and philosophical currents of their day, or the resolute marginalization of those who do the work of the theologian apart from the University: Francis de Sales, Bérulle, Fénelon.

Kant speaks of the conflict of faculties in a Protestant world; his discourse applies as well to a Catholic world. He speaks in a time of decadence for a Lutheran theology that was immersed, at the end of the Enlightenment, in the struggles that oppose rationalism and supernaturalism. But his argument is well and truly directed toward every university, every faculty of philosophy, and every faculty of theology. The new organon furnished by Galileo and Bacon announced the coming of the Enlightenment, and the end of the latter sees a triumph of science that will carry on: as witness to this triumph we can call to the stand the *Encyclopedia* of Diderot and Alembert. In such a context philosophy had the perfect means to defend its own scientificity—it is to this defense that Kant hastens by giving to the faculty of philosophy the place that pertained to the faculty of theology in the medieval University. The triumph of the Enlightenment is a philosophical triumph pasted over with the prestige of a priori or experimental science. However, theology did not truly have the resources to confer on itself the status of science. It is not always certain that it had the desire: the best contributions to theology that we owe to the eighteenth century are historical or philological and, for once, no one will contest the seriousness of the "positive" theology or of the biblical studies born in the Pietist milieu—a seriousness that merits being called "scholarly"[13] or "wissenschaftlich," though certainly not scientific in the new sense of the term. The rationalist theologians had certainly been capable of proposing a *theologia more geometrico demonstrata* destined to win renown for their faculty. The Catholic theologians had kept Scholasticism alive by shutting themselves within their faculty. After Kant the two positions are no longer tenable. Adaptation to the flavor of the day and its concepts is no longer tenable, first because (as always) the theologies thus produced quickly became dated, and second because the sole theology that had a right to a place in the University is no longer the one that takes advantage of the philosophies of the moment but the one that accepts the dictates of critical thought. (In the era of grand Scholasticism, the faculty of philosophy never practiced a politics of diktats and was content to be deeply annoyed by the treatment inflicted by the theologians on the Philosopher.) And a theology sticking to the positions that it occupied in the Middle Ages is no longer a viable theology: the Philosopher is now the master of only a few, the philosophers refuse more than in the Middle Ages to be put at the service of theology, and what survives of Scholasticism in the century of the Enlightenment coexists empirically with other disciplines of the University without any interdisciplinarity whatsoever. After the Enlightenment and Kant, Schleiermacher intervenes in time to shift the problematics and propose that theology is right at home in the University—but if here it is a science, it is in the sense of the German *Wissenschaft* and it will not take much for it to become a *Geisteswissenschaft*. Schleiermacher, translator of Plato, founder of modern hermeneutics and other services rendered to humanity, was very well placed, at the University of Berlin, to boldly defend the cultural role of theology. But when it became a matter of delivering the panegyric for the Confession of Augsburg in 1831, it was done regionally, within the walls of the faculty of theology, and the solemn ("secular") elegy was the work of a professor from the faculty of philosophy, namely Hegel. It is from now on philosophy's job to defend and exemplify Lutheranism . . .

Even Hegel proposed a philosophy capable of bringing to an end the "conflict of the faculties," to the degree, simply, that it absorbed the content of theology and carried it to a superior level of rationality. The price to pay was clearly high. In Hegel and the old Schelling, the theology that is appropriated by philosophy survives this appropriation only in its status as precursor to philosophy (Hegel) or as material offered up to philosophical work (Schelling). Despite their common past in pastoral training, neither Hegel nor Schelling is ever interested in the *rudes* or *vetula* dear to Gilson. Philosophy, wherever it exists, serves the *intellectus fidei*. But it does it by overflowing faith—the experience to which it leads by the hand is a philosophical experi-ence that is uniquely philosophical. The history of Idealist and post-Idealist theology is complex and does not interest us here. The theological Hegelianism that could interest us is that of the twentieth century, in which Hegel occupies a position near that of Aristotle at the beginning of the University. What must inter-est us, however, are the protests that it provoked. Kierkegaard and Barth should be mentioned here. Barth retained one duty from his years as a pastor: working toward a theology that could be preached. (The work was executed in part: not only is the kerygmatic character of the two commentaries on the Epistle to the Romans crystal clear, but even the *Dogmatics*, a scholarly work if there ever was one, does not forget to be led by a keryg-matic and homiletic project.) Kierkegaard preached only three times from the pulpit, but a considerable portion of his writings consists of "edifying discourses" and biblical meditations, which place him within the line of preacher theologians of antiquity and the Middle Ages. What does it mean to have a theology that can be preached, and, even more, ought to be? Above all it means a theology that takes leave of the School theologies (even if Barth had a long university career). There is more to say, and Kierkegaard ought to serve as the model more than Barth: not only is he a preacher (from his study), but also all of his theo-retical work shatters the university distribution of tasks. Are the *Philosophical Fragments* philosophical or theological? Is the common distinction between the philosophical and theologi-cal still there when we attempt to interpret the Kierkegaardian corpus? Obviously not. Kierkegaard did not teach, which spared him from choosing a clearly delimited "domain." There is even more to say. For if Kierkegaard appears in the history of thought as an "independent" (a cross-bencher),[14] it is perhaps in order to prove that the Scholastic and post-Scholastic distinction of roles, of the philosopher and the theologian, is mostly artificial. And if this is the case, then we must also admit that any idea of a "conflict of faculties" disappears, on the one hand, when we no longer know exactly where theology starts and philosophy ends and vice versa, and, on the other hand, when a text that includes authentic contributions to theology (the young Barth knew how to take advantage of this) is written without respect for the university division of labor. Scholasticism and its posterity lived by a certainty: theology was only theology and philosophy was only philosophy. After Kierkegaard, it is not certain (and perhaps also after Newman, his contemporary, whose *Grammar of Assent* is as much philosophical as it is theological) that this certainty is still justified. The scholarly character of the *Dogmatics* prohibits us from calling Barth a post-Scholastic theologian—and he stuck to a rigid distinction between philosophy and theology. Yet to speak of a post-Scholasticism in relation to Kierkegaard has every appearance of being right. Both the reorganization of the field that philosophy and theology occupied in a separated manner, and a reorganization of theological work itself, are probably the major (and largely unperceived) traits of a University where small and inevitable quarrels are the external appearance and the liquidation of the conflict of faculties is the fundamental phenomenon. And there is a strong chance that Kierkegaard therefore, who wanted to be neither theologian nor philosopher but a simply "Christian thinker," was the first witness to a theoretical work that is totally finished with a separation that has not borne any good fruit.

Let us explain this for fear of appearing to hold an historical misinterpretation. It is always good to recall some primary evidence: a non-Scholastic theology existed during the centuries when the theology of the School reigned. Bossuet was a preacher and a theologian. When he too was no longer a professor, Francis de Sales was a spiritual author (a convenient label), but above all a theologian in his own right. In these two cases we are dealing with some exceptions, and it is disturbing that we have the right to use the word. What are we proving by these exceptions and a thousand others except that an entire section of theology (that theology called "spiritual") was absent from the University? Even worse, these exceptions could be in danger. The loss of every organic link between theology and preaching from the Middle Ages to post-Tridentine Catholicism makes preaching an activity that theology ought to supervise, but from the outside. On the other hand, as soon as they exist independently of university discourse, spiritual theology or spiritual writing can lead to the stake (Marguerite Porete) or the dungeon (John of the Cross, despite his irreproachable university past), or more modestly (but very often) can attract the attention of the inquisitors. Furthermore, the appearance of a discipline called "spiritual theology" suggests that there is a nonspiritual theology—about which it will never be said that it is done solely for the pleasure of knowledge—its texts can also exude boredom—but about which it must be admitted that it is scholarly and only scholarly. The last great theologians to have written for the University and outside of it were without doubt Bonaventure and Eckhart. In the thirteenth century a single doctor was still capable of commenting on the *Sentences* and writing the *Itinerarium*. A little after him the same theologian and professor was capable of composing an oeuvre with two faces, Latin treatises and German sermons (in such a way that the sermons are not the vulgarization of the treatises but rather the continuation of the same work by other means). This was no longer possible in the following centuries—and the greatest thinker in the Latin world before Luther, Nicholas of Cusa, was outside of the university world. Therefore as soon as the concept of "spiritual theology" appears, or at least when the label is applied, one starts to tremble. The unity of theological work is lost as soon as theology defined itself (and was defined) as a university discipline, when it pretends to reign over the University, or when it wants to conserve its hard-won place. This unity is lost as soon as theology is handed university work as its first task and the theologian has no other role to play than a "scientific" kind. There is certainly nothing to say about the spiritual life of the theologian of the School: Thomas Aquinas gives every appearance of being rightly declared a saint, whereas Cyril of Alexandria was truly not a saint . . . In any case a ditch was created between the end of the pre-university schools and the theology of the School, and between the "scientific" work of the theologian and his duty toward preaching and spiritual teaching. (Some spiritual teaching still exists in the Scholastic manuals. But it is a spiritual teaching for students as such.) The theologian, moreover, had no other dialogue partner for his "scientific" work than philosophy—and a philosophy that was evidently no longer there in order to console him if necessary and had no official function but to furnish him with conceptual instruments.

Can theology then be satisfied with bearing the two titles of "science" and non-philosophy? That which is played out in the fittingly termed post-Scholastic period, of which Kierkegaard is certainly a foundational figure, is played out in the answer one gives to this question. The philosopher and the theologian will not know who they are or what their task is unless their relation is rethought and reorganized. Despite the few questions that we have raised in passing, it is undeniable that this has not yet happened—after all, Neo-Scholasticism is still alive and well.

THREE

Philosophy, Theology, and the Task of Thinking

We can affirm without any shilly-shallying that Scholastic theology is a *scientia*. And because the University was *universitas scientiarum*, we can propose the equivalence of *scientia* and university discipline. This suffices for the epoch. This will also suffice later, after the appearance of the concept of science, if we are content to assign to theology a place among the various kinds of knowledge (knowledge does not mean science) handed on in the University. These various kinds of knowledge are not necessarily sciences in the modern sense of the term. Philology, history, the critical reading of texts, are all a matter of knowledge without being a matter of science. They are certainly "sciences" if we refer to the vast semantic field of the German *Wissenschaft*. And if we do, we can always appeal to the distinction between the "sciences of nature" (to which it is necessary to tie the a priori sciences, logic and mathematics) and the "sciences of the spirit" in order to find the most appropriate niche in which to place theological work. Schleiermacher's response to the scientism of the Enlightenment ineluctably led here. On the one hand, there is a positivity to Christianity, a "Christian fact" about which we can speak in a "scientific" manner (*geisteswissenschaftlich*): we can write about and interpret its history. On the other hand, there is a positivity to Christian experience, and for want of speaking *in recto* about the Absolute to which it claims to adhere, we can always scrutinize this experience and interpret theology as a science of experience (for lack of being an experiment: a psychology of religious experience, and finally of Christian experience, will serve here as the unshakable foundation). The theology of this sort is nothing less than a "science of the spirit." (And it becomes the work of the understanding, *verstehen*, for lack of being able to be explained, *erklären*.) In Schleiermacher and his century, theology explains to cultivated minds, then to believers interested in understanding their faith, what they can believe and what they do when they believe. Theology therefore rightfully remains an academic discipline (which does not prohibit it from being banished from universities every now and then). To define it as *scientia* is impossible after the Galilean and Baconian revolution, unless we were to translate *scientia* as discipline. In Hegelian terms the word can mean an "experience of consciousness." The realization of such an experience is a "science" in German, but in German alone. However, it is not a science for those who from now on oversee the meaning of this word and the totality of scientific practices. And this could suffice to redefine in a new context the relation of theology and philosophy—less numerous, after all, are the philosophical enterprises that claim scientific legitimacy.[1]

Let us mention as a sort of preliminary the effort of T. F. Torrance, as brilliant as it is moving.[2] Could theology, despite everything, be counted among the sciences? Torrance's tactic in what he does not hesitate to call a "philosophy of theology," and refuses to call simply a theological epistemology, is seductive. "After all"—after the modern concept of science is imposed, theology could very well satisfy the requirements of this concept. Modernity has produced an entity or two, first the "object," then the "fact." Theology itself appeals to facts, let us say phenomena, and its mission is to let them appear as such starting from themselves—a possible definition of objectivity. The normative concept, science, is only present in the plurality of sciences, thus in the plurality of modes of objectivity and of our ways of reaching an agreement with objectivity. But if one admits that there is a general theory of scientific knowledge or

FROM THEOLOGY TO THEOLOGICAL THINKING

a universal model of scientificity, and Torrance does it without reserve, then the modern discrediting of theology could very well not be scientific because it bypasses a fundamental mode of objectivity, that of the revealed God, and of a fundamental mode of knowledge that we reserve for this revelation. *Theological Science* pleads for the scientific character of theology, not by leading its method back to this or that other scientific discipline, but by manifesting the adequacy of what theology knows and the manner by which it is known.[3] Theology (and here we are in the wake of Barth and at the antipodes of Schleiermacher) has its object, its *positum*, and the object is not what we say or feel about God, but what God says or gives to be felt. And Torrance concedes to Heidegger, whom he has not read, that positivity is the common lot of physics and theology.[4] The distinct object has a distinct welcome in consciousness and a distinct welcome in knowledge and its discourse. However, the distinction creates no hiatus. It is doubtful that the same kind of knowledge is shared between learning the words of the other and learning the words of the Other with a capital O. Nothing assures us that we are dealing with knowledge in a univocal way in both cases. Yet the rub is found when we realize that while Torrance is speaking of laws that govern any knowledge faithful to its object, he inevitably neglects the constitutive traits of science in its Galilean and Baconian model: mathematization, verification, testing [*contrôle*], and prediction. Theology verifies only in a minimal way with philological or historical verifications. It does not experiment: what it speaks about escapes all mastery [*contrôle*]. If it predicts, it is only in a tenuous mode—thus the believer predicts that, all things being equal, a little bread and wine will be in certain circumstances signs of a certain presence in a certain place. And is it at all useful to deny that theology undertakes no work of mathematization? A science that does not verify (one can speak of eschatological verification,[5] but this will be for lack of better words and to confess a historical impossibility), that does not test, and whose predictions are realized only for the believer—and not for whoever has eyes to see[6]—

such a science contradicts the modern canons of scientificity. Torrance's goal is to authorize theology to take its seat at the table of the sciences (in the modern sense of the term) without embarrassment. It seems that his most important result is to have shown, despite himself, that theology could serve as a critical authority for post-Baconian and post-Galilean science. Theology lets God speak and does not constrain him to speak. It predicts neither what he will say nor what he will do. And no mathematization is of the least use to it . . .

A second attempt should be summoned to the witness stand. When science is established as the model for legitimate knowledge, can philosophy itself assume the title of science? It has been capable of doing so. With Husserl it has even been capable of presenting itself not only as rigorous science but even as the only science worthy of the name. At the end of his oeuvre, Husserl examines a crisis of the sciences and signals that only phenomenology (his) can put an end to this crisis by updating the relation of the "lifeworld" and the "scientific world." But if Husserl's phenomenology lacks anything but rigor, at what price do we give it the name of science? Here again the German can mislead us: *Wissenschaft* does not exactly mean science, in French or in English, but designates more broadly a labor ordered toward knowledge. For the Vienna Circle phenomenology is evidently a non-science in every sense of the term. For the one who reads Husserl honestly, it is in fact more than a science: constituted as architectonic knowledge, and even as the sole knowledge which, starting from below (the expression often reappears in the Master's correspondences), can lead all the way up to God, phenomenology is the science on which all the others rest and which can therefore critique them all. Phenomenology is not absolute knowledge [*savoir*], a definitive and unsurpassable content of experiential knowledge [*connaissance*]. But it has the right to pass for absolute science: the sure method, after Descartes but without being preoccupied with Bacon (Husserl knows only Galileo), that can preside over the organization of all knowledge worthy of the name, whether to legitimate it from a distance (thus when one asks after the origin of geometry) or in order to produce it (thus when one proceeds to map the vast continent of consciousness). However, is there a univocal usage of the word "science" between phenomenology (or philosophy) as science and physics as science? Just as one can doubt this in relation to Torrance, so also to Husserl. Phenomenology is proposed as a general theory of knowledge [*connaissance*], while theology, in Torrance, is a kind of knowledge [*connaissance*] as rigorous as any other. Setting it apart from theology, phenomenology has no proper domain: anything that can be described belongs to it by right. (But it has its own field, that of consciousness.) But, admitting this right to describe everything, is his phenomenological practice "scientific" in the present sense of the term, that is, ever since science took over for *scientia*? This could be the case. But it is the case only when one adopts a conception of science that is not that issued from the tradition of Bacon. (Recall that Bacon is absent from the pages of the *Crisis*, which know only Galileo as the father of modern science.) Phenomenology certainly has the advantage over theology in being experimental—it suffices to mention here the theory of variations, which is incontestably a matter of controlled experiment [*expérience*] and which allows verification and prediction into its order. In exploring its "field," the "terrain of consciousness," phenomenology, and this is what matters, is placed above every other science (it is an *epistēmē* as well as an epistemology). It does not impose its method on all other sciences, even if it proposes it to some: there cannot be a phenomenological physics or phenomenological mathematics, even if there can be a sociology (or a theology for that matter) submitted to the influence of phenomenology.[7] And in fundamentally being both a philosophy endowed with a domain and a metascience, phenomenology cannot exactly pretend to be *a* science. By suggesting that it founds *the* science par excellence, Husserl in fact takes leave of the modern concept of scientificity. The sciences in crisis that concern the *Crisis* are only sciences. Phenomenology thus takes leave of the modern concept of science all together.

One will therefore dare to say, albeit with a degree of caution, that theology and philosophy are not sciences. It ought to be clear, in saying this, that we do not proceed to a negation. Theology and philosophy are non-sciences only according to the model of knowledge [*connaissance*] of the Logical Positivists: a model that only knows, on the one hand, some positive elements of knowledge [*des saviors*] and, on the other, an a priori science, logic, the good use of which will allow (in theory) the integration of all particular knowledge into the whole of a "unified science." Yet theology and philosophy are not sciences, in a nonreductive sense, if we admit that their use of the *logos* overflows that of mathematics or biology. It would be necessary to concede to Torrance that theology is not less than scientific and to Adriaanse that phenomenological rigor is a close neighbor to theological rigor.[8] And we can now leave the last word to Heidegger. In the late lecture published as "Phenomenology and Theology," the concept of "positive" science dominates (a science that pertains to one single object). Here theology is one positive science among the totality (the science of God or faith), while philosophy asks after the totality without any restriction imposed by limits—the sole boundary that it could recognize, though Heidegger does not say it, is that between (as one chooses) being and non-being or being and the beyond being. Theology certainly is "positive," but Heidegger recognized later on that it is so in a way "totally other" than the other sciences.[9] However, is it necessary to maintain the break admitted by Heidegger between philosophical work and theological work? There are some reasons not to. (a) A first, very small reason is provided by what we can reject (despite everything!): the "scientific" character, in the German sense, of both kinds of work. Their comembership in the totality of university disciplines was a modern, or protomodern, fate. This fate was dire. Yet theology survived—which is proven by the facts. Philosophy, on the other hand, certainly no longer has the intention of serving theology, but it just as certainly has no more intention of governing it either. And if one has enough circumspection not to speak too often about "science," a certain proximity between them is what will make us think.

The particularity of a discipline (bracketing the "question of being") is that it is regional: the mathematician is not concerned with subatomic particles. It is also a particularity of a discipline, however, to have frontiers and to come across frontier problems. The mathematician is not interested in subatomic particles, but the physicist needs mathematics in order to model the behavior of the aforementioned particles. And it is not necessary to push much further to see that the "positum" proper to theology, however one defines it, seriously interests the philosopher, and that the philosophical set of questions and responses is of course not unimportant to the theologian. It so happens that the theologian is his own philosopher to himself. In the twentieth century Barth and Balthasar were able to borrow few concepts and forged for themselves the majority of the concepts that they used: the Balthasarian concept of "form" is not borrowed (it is difficult to uncover its genealogy); the Barthian theology of creation and covenant borrows from no one its foundational concept, etc. These often radically autonomous theologies are the exception. And because the theologian is a "scholar" (not a scientist but a *savant*), we ought to extend him the courtesy of believing him capable of reading philosophical texts, and of reading them in a critical manner, and of letting them render some service to theology. Surely it is one thing to forge a concept and another to make use of one. But must we believe that the work of instrumentalization, well or poorly carried out, leaves wholly intact the concept instrumentalized? It would be naive. The Averroist philosophers of the Sorbonne were scandalized (in a strictly philosophical way) when their theologian colleagues, their neighbors, made use of a monstrous concept, transubstantiation, to articulate the Eucharistic conversion. They were right: in Aristotelian terms, one substance cannot be substituted for another without affecting the accidents of the first substance. They were also right because the theologians who proceeded in this way made explicit appeal to the Aristotelian theory of substance and its accidents. However, the scandal ceases when one realizes that the concepts of substance and accident are borrowed, by Thomas Aquinas and others, for reasons of pure convenience that have nothing to do with a supposed fidelity to Aristotle. (And the scandal totally disappears when theology simply keeps to the concept of transubstantiation, at least because of the approval it received from the Catholic hierarchy, and no longer bears the least interest in any other substance or attributes than these.) In any case, the discussion is one among scholars. And if it should have an end it will be—as has been the case—in creating the conditions for an even more advanced interrogation of substance. The philosopher and the theologian work in their own faculties, but these faculties have a common frontier. And if it is almost certain that after Hegel, Schelling, and Kierkegaard, briefly, after the well-considered departure from the Enlightenment in the masters of the nineteenth century, each can inhabit his faculty without ignoring the existence of this frontier zone where the destiny of theology as much as philosophy is sometimes played out. Let us reiterate: in the same University today, philosophy and theology can be practiced only after Hegel, Schelling, and Kierkegaard. The "conflict of the faculties" is over. And if the chemist and the theologian are constrained, perhaps, to converse politely, the soft paradigm of conversation no longer applies in those cases where one can learn from the other and where some cause others to think. (b) We are just beginning a discussion that is a little more interesting than that of a "conflict of the faculties." According to Heidegger, philosophy speaks about everything and theology speaks only about its proper object (God or faith). But if one point is certain, it is that, despite Heidegger, philosophy cannot fail, and has never failed, to ask about the objects that are the supposedly exclusive property of theology. There are some philosophies without theological interest. The philosopher of mathematics rarely comes up against that about which the theologian speaks (except when he speaks of a mathematical infinite in act and is obliged to explain to the theologian that the divine infinite is not the only infinite in act—but since Cantor, the theologians have learned this . . .). Since Lucretius there have been atheist philosophies. But after Kant, the philosophical project that should hold our attention a little more than the others is the philosophy of revelation (already in Hegel and then in Schelling and also in Kierkegaard, though we do not have to take sides here in favor of one or another). Modern theology has made "revelation" one of its master concepts. This concept is not necessarily the same in its theological and philosophical uses, and it possesses more than one philosophical usage: "revelation" patently does not mean the same thing in Hegel and Rosenzweig. In any case the fact that a classic thesis was consecrated to Hegel's Trinitarian theology and did not provoke an objection is a symptom that neither can nor ought to pass by unnoticed.[10] More dramatically, Xavier Tilliette's concept of "philosophical Christology" warns us that the *Logos* par excellence, the Word of God, can be made (and has been made) the object of a discourse that intends to be philosophical or, more modestly, comes from the faculty of philosophy.[11] To push this even further, let us ask what it means to philosophize after Kierkegaard. We will be told that he practices non-philosophy more than philosophy.[12] Perhaps one is right to say this. But, having said it, it will be necessary to concede without delay that the concept of non-philosophy is a concept of philosophical origin, forged in order to name a line of demarcation (between "philosophy" and the "religious"), and that the concept possesses an unjustified violence. Kierkegaard wanted to articulate Christianity. He wanted to do so through concepts and in his edifying discourses, which are texts that are assuredly non-philosophical. And where he wanted to do it through concepts, in his pseudonymous works, he could only proceed by way of a constant back and forth between work that is properly philosophical (thus his critique of the Hegelian dialectic in the name of Aristotelian *kinesis*) and strictly theological (thus his theory of the almost total incognito of the God made man whose identity is only perceived by an act of love). It would be artificial to demarcate philosophy and theology. In Kierkegaard the philosophical is not non-theological. The theological—this is always the case in the pseudonymous works—is never non-philosophy pure and simple. The work is philosophical and theological at once. Unless, of course, it is neither one nor the other . . . (c) The reasons are therefore clear why it is useless for us to hold on to the language of scientificity. Regarding Kierkegaard again, Heidegger, half-polemically, half-judiciously, remarked that the edifying discourses represent the richest piece of his oeuvre, with the exception of *The Concept of Anxiety*.[13] Perhaps this was to annex the pseudonymous works too quickly to the classic field of philosophy—we just said that they do not truly belong to it. But Heidegger also recognized, to which we can only give our consent, that the distinction of the philosophical (or theological) and the "spiritual" ceases, on the one hand, to have value in light of a corpus like Kierkegaard's, and, on the other hand, that no one can be a philosopher anymore, in 1927, if he does not recognize the weight of the spiritual texts. Kierkegaard does not propose a theory in his edifying discourses. Resuming a distinction we already analyzed, these texts emanate from a *theōria*. Furthermore, *theōria* is an attitude toward things that is as antiscientific as possible. It does not measure, does not control, does not predict. We let be what we contemplate. Our admiration can be transformed into praise. In every case it is never given the means to dominate. What philosophy or theology "knows" is never in doubt (even if there are philosophical and theological misinterpretations and ignorance . . .). However, knowledge is not science. And when we cannot exactly say "where" we are, whether in a philosophical or theological field, nor say precisely what we are "doing," whether a philosophical or theological work, wisdom requires us to say that the rigor of our knowledge is often making the best of an excess in relation to all scientificity or a withdrawal from it (as one chooses). There is certainly a place in philosophy, and, why not, in theology, for properly scientific work: we have the right to formalize and to resort to the most constraining procedures of logic. For example, the phi-

FROM THEOLOGY TO THEOLOGICAL THINKING

losophy of science cannot totally dispense with being scientific. The work of the philosopher and theologian, however, are not confined in the same way. A philosophy or theology that is only a science would be erecting theories without taking the necessary delay of *theōria*. To deny that philosophy and theology are merely sciences (without believing that they are less than science) comes down to taking this delay. And this leads us back to two things: subordinating theory to *theōria* and refusing any hasty distinction between the philosophical, the theological, and the spiritual.

The dossier for "spiritual" literature therefore needs to be reopened. As we mentioned above, a tragedy occurred, the appearance of a theology called "spiritual," which was endowed with a certain academic independence. Further, set as an appendix to dogmatic or systematic theology, spiritual theology could speak only in last place. We know that the "spiritual writer" comes on stage after the theologian proper, and that his status will always remain uncertain. As taught at the University, spiritual theology will always be mediocre—unimaginative. The spiritual thinkers, if only they would write and speak, will always be better masters than the professors of spiritual theology ("ascetic and mystical" theology in the Catholic tradition). Spirituality is certainly not a-theological, and Catholicism has recognized this by counting among its doctors such "theologians" as Teresa of Avila or Thérèse of Lisieux, neither of whom possessed the least bit of technical formation in theology, but who no less had a doctrine to transmit (*expressis verbis* in Thérèse of Lisieux). (Sacred) "doctrine" is the name of theology until the beginning of Scholasticism. In a certain sense, the theology of both Teresas, and of a thousand other women and men, takes a step back out of Scholasticism. Doctors have not been professors. But what does it mean to teach? Those to whom we allude here were certainly teachers, and they taught both their religious brothers and sisters and their readers. Spiritual theology is a fruit of Scholastic decadence. Spirituality is in part the fruit of a relation of teaching lived outside the schools, and in part—

it is necessary to acknowledge—a fruit of the invention of the printing house. We speak of schools of spirituality—Rhineland-Flemish spirituality, Carmelite spirituality, Bérullian spirituality—and the unity of place is often lost for the sake of a more fluid but real unity of those who recognize in the words, oral or printed, a spiritual master who teaches without professing. The spiritual master can have disciples—but his teaching first takes the form of "spiritual direction." He can also exercise his influence by means of the book. And in both cases, the classroom disappears. The professor of spiritual theology in the university will comment on the texts of the spiritual writers and attempt to give them coherence, even inscribing them into the history of theology *tout court* (hence the integration of John of the Cross into the history of Thomism under the preeminent influence of Garrigou-Lagrange). But he himself will rarely be a spiritual master—his mode of life and work will not be favorable to it. And all this did not fall short of harming a university teaching in which spirituality no longer occurred but in the form of a codicil.

Spirituality is not a science and has never pretended to be. And when a spiritual author speaks about a "science of the cross," let us not be deceived by her words.[14] Linking its history, or at least its recent history, to the appearance of a philosophy and/or theology that refuses all scientific character (Kierkegaard's *Postscriptum* is called "nonscientific," which may signify more than a protest arising from an encounter with Hegel and German Idealism more generally) allows us to specify what we are talking about. Theology does not respond to the Baconian or Galilean criteria of scientificity, and it is not to be moved by them. We could appeal to other criteria of scientificity, as in Torrance, in order to organize a debate about the fidelity of a "subject" to its "object" or of consciousness to that which enters its field, etc. But should we truly consider scientificity as a criterion of respectability? Or should we not observe that science, after all, is only science? We speak of *theōria* in order to distinguish it from theories that are only its sedimentation. In its Greek origins, is *theōria* a scientific or prescientific work?

To respond, let us appeal to a recent opinion, Heidegger's. (a) The opinion is first wrapped up within a negative formula that we should not read too quickly: "science does not think."[15] The minor scandal that it arouses is inevitably irrelevant. Philosophy does not consider "thinking" an equivalent to cogitating. Like every human enterprise, science or the sciences involve us as animals capable of cogitating: even the person who has "lost his mind" cogitates, and we cease cogitating only when we lose consciousness or when consciousness sleeps. If we admit the equivalency of cogitation and thought, scientific work would clearly be the work of thought, and it would be totally pointless to distinguish the work of the mathematician, of the philosopher, and of the one who prays, thinking of God by loving him. How, then, in a sense, does one not think? (b) To respond, we will ask: what is this authority, "science," about which it is said that it does not think? What is this work, "thought," to which it is not open? In Heidegger, science is defined by a work, the mathematization of being in its totality, as such alone capable of making verification, control, and prediction reign. This, and only this, is science. Again, its work is "mental": who would deny it? This work is equally heuristic. Science, not content merely to master, also does the work of discovery. But once these first truths are conceded, that which Heidegger's formula tells us is still poorly understood. Science lives out of an ambition and a capacity: to structure mathematically everything that is. But, we ask, is this all there is to do in order to get to know the totality of being? The shortest phenomenological description (and, no doubt, descriptions other than the phenomenological) allows us to respond negatively. Not only is there a reality that is not mathematizable, or of which we would lose the exact sense if we want to submit it to mathematization, but also what we cannot mathematize is perhaps the most important. It is possible to articulate the *Pietà* of Michelangelo through equations. But having done this, we have rendered an account not of a work of art but of an object analogous to every other object. We have performed a mental work, just as the physicist specializing in meteorology performs a mental work. (Yet already our equations themselves possess an undeniable artistic value.) However, the physicist describes in order to predict. To describe the statue mathematically, on the other hand, has no other end in sight than to demonstrate our mathematical competency—and the statue is merely the occasion to demonstrate it. (c) "Science does not think" should also be understood starting from another Heideggerian affirmation, the subordination of science to technology. At its origin, science is tied to *theōria*. At its zenith, however, its criterion of validity is utility. Scientific discoveries have occurred that cannot be technologically applied: thus non-Euclidean geometries, which in the time of Riemann or Lobachevsky "served" no purpose at all. But even if the a priori sciences are able to propose results that are not immediately utilizable, it seems as if, in the twentieth century, the utilizable had become the criterion of scientificity. Nowadays we use non-Euclidean geometries to model the space-time of Einsteinian physics. We imagine experiences capable of demonstrating the paradoxes of theoretical physics. There is more: the a priori sciences nourish the experimental sciences, but the experimental sciences are not the last word on science, which is in fact accomplished when it can be utilized—science is therefore, according to Heidegger, a tool in service to technology. A concept, then, brings to a conclusion the Heideggerian critique of science and technology, "enframing," or *Gestell*. In the beginning was *theōria*; in the end is domination. *Theōria*, which is bound up with contemplation, lets be and neither produces nor masters anything. It does not produce. We could also say that it does the work of description and not construction—and therefore that it can be neither destroyed nor deconstructed. However, it can be forgotten: the reign of technology is just such a forgetting. But can we say that *theōria* "thinks," in contrast to a modern science that does not? This needs to be investigated.

The investigation is not difficult. Heidegger tells us that science does not think. But who, according to the philosopher, does think? True to say, no one; thought is introduced in Heidegger as that which we do not yet do. What should be thought most of all, he says in a lecture course of 1931–32, is the fact that we do not yet think.[16] What does this mean? The course continues with a commentary on a word of Nietzsche about the advent of nihilism: "the desert grows." And the conclusion imposes itself: thought, if it comes, will allow us to traverse unharmed the time of nihilism. How? Heidegger is prudent enough to say little about thought. He defines it negatively: philosophy is coming to its end and thought is called to survive this end. He defines it normatively: the order of thought is not that of fact but of task. This is not sufficient. And in the lecture course of 1931–32 a terminological and conceptual link is posed between *denken*, thinking, and *danken*, thanking or giving thanks. In 1953 technology appears as *Gestell*, thought already having appeared as *Gedanc*, another neologism, and the two concepts are probably linked despite the temporal break. Is thought tied to thanking as technology will be tied to enframing? More trenchantly, is thought the work of thanking as technology is the work of domination? Is the truth of what happens in the world manifested in *Gedanc* and *Gestell*? The texts do not prohibit us from saying this. There is certainly a difference: technological domination happens, and it does so before our very eyes, whereas thought still awaits the favorable time of its coming (which, doubtlessly, can only be near, and tied to the work of Heidegger). But both of these, and it is this that should weigh most heavily, are the secret of an epoch—one, the last word of the present, the other, the inaugural word of the future. In the time of nihilism we do not yet think. As soon as we do think, we will have dissipated nihilism.

And it is this relation to the future that we cannot concede too quickly. Is thought merely a labor for today and tomorrow? To respond in the affirmative, we would certainly not say up front that we have forgotten everything until today—"everything," that is, everything that matters. We will say instead that if there is something un-thought, the reign of metaphysics has left it un-thought. The task of thinking arises when the reign of metaphysics comes to an end—and let us be precise—when the time of metaphysics is closed. The task of thinking is hinted at in one moment of history and not another. (A little dramatically, and we hope involuntarily, Heidegger risks passing himself off as the first person who has tried to think . . .) The end of metaphysics, nihilism as the time of the "desert," and the task of thinking are all linked together. But is it truly necessary to await the time of the desert for the task of thinking to become manifest? The quotation from Nietzsche on which Heidegger relies continues with some significant words: "woe to him who conceals deserts within." The quotation is dated, and the woe that it is talking about is equally dated. Nietzsche speaks of a nihilism rapping at the gate in 1885, Heidegger speaks about it in 1931, and they are speaking to us about a reality inscribed within their timelines. Is nihilism unknown before 1885? Is the end of metaphysics an event contemporary with Heidegger? We doubt it. If the history of philosophy is a history of metaphysics, you would have to prove that it is only a history of metaphysics—and counterexamples are not lacking.[17] If nihilism reigns at the very moment when metaphysics seems to be crumbling down all at once, it is not in the sense of a new arrival, as in Nietzsche, but (at least in virtue of the theory of the eternal return) rather something like an ever-present possibility. Is nihilism always secretly there? Reciprocally, have there then always been those able to take their leave of metaphysics? To think and (or in order) to traverse nihilism—what Heidegger tells us is perfectly clear. Yet it is still the case that the experience of nihilism is not only ours but also others' before us, and also that, after all, the experience of thinking is ancient. In stating that "we do not yet think," Heidegger literally denies that we have always already thought or that others besides us have done so. "Thought," therefore, arises in what we will have to call a philosophy of history, at the twilight of one history and in anticipation of a "new beginning."[18] The episodes that succeed each other are not numerous: metaphysics receives its classical form in Thomas Aquinas,[19] it is associated with the mathematization of being in its totality, it is accomplished in Nietzsche, the last metaphysician, and then the double domination of nihilism and technology arrives. But we should not concede all of this without reflecting on it. Both the perennial possibility of nihilism and of a philosophy without collusion with metaphysics ought to be taken with equal seriousness. The secret of nihilism is that the highest values are devaluated and it is with the death of God that metaphysics accomplished its supreme value. God is dead, and the highest values are devaluated because they could be. Did nihilism wait until 1885 to rap at the gate? Affirming its possibility allows us to respond negatively. Is technology a moment in our history? Here again, the reality is truly conceivable only by being led back to the possible: the possibility of *Gestell* is inscribed in our relation to reality. And consequently, does thought have no other reality than in the future? Here again, we are compelled to affirm a possibility as old as philosophy itself and, who knows, even older. Some years before Heidegger, a more sensible proposal was made by Rosenzweig, in an essay entitled "The New Thinking."[20] For Rosenzweig thinking has a history. And after German Idealism and the First World War, the time has come to think otherwise or in a fresh way. What does this mean? It means essentially the same thing that Heidegger will say a little later: the reblending of thought and praise, a nonobjectifying and nonscientific thinking. If there is no proof that Heidegger read Rosenzweig, there is certainly no proof that he did not ("The New Thinking" dates from 1925). Good sense suggests that we see here an involuntary convergence, which is more important than some unconfessed influence would be. Rosenzweig dedicated his first great work to Hegel.[21] For him it is self-evident that Hegel is a thinker. However, Rosenzweig had the ambition of bringing Hegelianism to an end—*The Star of Redemption* is one of the most brilliant demolitions of Hegel that we have. The assigned task is clear: thinking after Hegel and thinking against him (which was already the goal of Kierkegaard, and it has not been observed enough that his tactic is near that of Rosenzweig's). But the one who is tacitly assigned this task admits that the work of thinking has existed before the project of a new thinking was formed. He admits that others thought before us.

It is henceforth wise to be newly troubled about theological work. It is clear that in Rosenzweig theology (supposing we can use the term in relation to a Jewish thought) also takes part in the genesis of a new thinking. It is equally clear that in Heidegger theology is not it either—theological overtones are not lacking in the course of 1931–32, nor even one or two theological allusions; theology perhaps gives rise to thought, but the text does not genuinely say that it thinks. The fact remains, and Heidegger knew this well, that theology at its best always wants to give thanks or to praise. Yet it is not sufficient to give thanks in order to think: one will freely concede to every objection from Heidegger.

Nevertheless the most superficial reading of the entire theological corpus of the East, the Greeks, and the Latins ties intellectual work and the work of praise in such a way as to allow a daring hypothesis. Could it be that theology is playing the same game as *Gedanc*? The theologian is certainly defined as the one who prays (in truth) before appearing as someone who "thinks" or claims to think. It is right to concede to Balthasar certainly that theology is ready to kneel before writing at a desk. Ideally, it should write while kneeling and, above all, its texts should not take God for an object but as interlocutor, whether as in Anselm, Augustine, or others. Of course, this is not enough. Theology speaks of God (and of all things *sub ratione Dei*). The theologian is a scholar—a *savant*—within the community of scholars. Even the most anxious scholar concerned with speaking "about" [*sur*] God, cannot avoid the inevitable traps of objectifying language.[22] However, a question ought to be posed: in the community of scholars, would not the theologian be the one whose work most evidently disposes him to thinking? We will develop this hypothesis. (a) An objection arises first: that the theologian belongs to a "community" of scholars is not so cut-and-dried (as it is not clear that such a community exists after knowledge becomes parceled out into specialties in such a way that the specialists can no longer have anything but a courteous conversation among themselves). However, the objection disappears when we see that after Gutenberg the theologian belongs to a community of readers and writers, which helps him avoid any ghettoization—without, of course, requiring everyone to be interested in theology, whether this occurs passively or actively. The medieval and pre-Scholastic models that we have mentioned, the monastic, cathedral, and canonical schools, universities in an embryonic state, certainly lived from a constant (and easily practiced) interdisciplinarity, and the conflict of the faculties arose from, among other things, a compartmentalization that prevented this interdisciplinarity. The blunders committed against "Anselm's proof" since Scholasticism prove this: in the monastic *studium* the blending of disciplines is common. And if we should be granted a wish for the University in its contemporary form, it would be double: on the one hand, that the conflict of the faculties be forgotten, and on the other, that the theologian and the philosopher be capable of reading each other's work and, if necessary, influencing one another. It is a commonplace that "the" scientific community no longer exists, broken up into scientific communities, in the plural, incapable of reading and influencing each other (even if some exceptions exist).[23] If this truth is to continue, then the theologian remains all alone, and his pretension to thinking in praising remains inaudible, or audible only to theologians—in which case the question of thinking would be posed in theology in a uniquely theological way. But should this truth truly be perpetuated? (b) If we argue that it should not be perpetuated, a new question simultaneously appears. Can we, in fact, mark out a theological field and a philosophical field? We can trace a nice line of demarcation between theology and mathematics (this does not prohibit a theological interest in the ontic status of mathematical objects). Yet between theology and philosophy everything seems as if we cannot. At the origins of (Christian) theology it is evident that the *logos* is the same in what we call philosophy and what we call theology—with the minor reservation that philosophy is an affair of love and that theology does not sign up for this affair under the same name. In the Scholastic organization of knowledge, on the other hand, this became not so evident. We are entitled to believe, however, that this organization is over and, therefore, that theology and philosophy are facing up to the same emergency, thinking in a post-Scholastic epoch in which the University has a greater need for independents or cross-benchers than for specialists in (as one chooses) "nature" or "supernature." The theologian does not speak about everything. He does speak about everything, however, in its relation to an Absolute whom he understands as creator, savior, and the one disposed to lead everything to completion. Others can also maintain an all-encompassing discourse: the "Christian gnosis" of Hegel is not exactly a theology by the book, but it does take hold of almost every object of theological discourse, from creation to eschatology, passing through sacramental theology.[24] Who will say that Hegel is not a theologian but his critic Staudenmaier is?[25] Intra-theological criteria exist: in the first place a theologian's belonging to a body of believers. The philosopher, however, can very well live, comfortably or uncomfortably, as a "Christian without Church,"[26] or as a Christian critical of every Church. On the other hand, these criteria impose some obligations on the theologian whose mission is meant to be "ecclesial."[27] But this does not mean that they should be seen as obstacles to the freedom of thinking. *Schriftgebundenheit*, *Konfessionsgebundenheit*, fidelity to the Magisterium in the Catholic tradition, etc.—these do not all demand that theology be only about theology and that philosophy be only about philosophy: both make decisions about what is given to them to think. It is by their works that we recognize thinkers, and not by their place in a Church or university. (c) The prudent abolition of boundaries and limits ought finally to be considered as a threefold task: for the equal good of the University, of theology, and of philosophy. The situation is conceivable in which thinking becomes an extra-university labor: when theology perpetuates in the University an obsolete division of knowledge, and when philosophy survives by making metaphysics survive. However, this situation is daunting. If the task to accomplish is the task of thinking—and not that of calculating reason, historiography, or others—then the task is incontestably new, as it is tied by Heidegger to the end of philosophy, understood as the end of onto-theo-logy, i.e., of metaphysics. But we have some old means for dealing with this new task. Again, the idea of a new task and of an end of metaphysics is certainly daunting: Heidegger, content with elementary indications, does not describe the task in detail, and the end of metaphysics for him is still a project for which, after Heidegger, we still only have some elementary indications. And we do not see clearly where and how one could (or has been able to) begin this task. The name of postmodernity, for example, did not truly designate a new "condition," but rather a new moment in modern times; the fate of those who wanted to think in a postmodern way was inevitably to call white on black what was formerly called black on white. We can keep the concept, however, under one condition: its linkage with nihilism. Indeed nihilism, the sort that in any event we experience (actual nihilism, therefore, and not the perpetually possible kind), plunges its roots into modernity. If we accept the linkage of its destiny to that of science and technology, then nihilism is what brings them to completion. This completion seems to leave us powerless. But in appearance only. In Nietzsche only the will to power, as art of creating values, can overcome nihilism. In Heidegger thought possesses this power. And if, sometime after the course consecrated to thinking, Heidegger affirms the end of philosophy and entrusts to us a new, post-philosophical, post-metaphysical task, then it would seem to be necessary to assign to theology and philosophy, whatever the names we give them, the common task of thinking—and therefore of thinking without boundaries. Every age lives in crisis, and the crisis in which we live finds one of its best diagnostics outside the Heideggerian analysis of the end of metaphysics in Balthasar, particularly in the conclusion to *Herrlichkeit* III/2.[28] These pages, dedicated to "Our Inheritance and the Christian Task," serve as a coda to a long itinerary traveled through the history of metaphysics, where poets, mystics, philosophers, and theologians are equally summoned. The journey ends with an official statement: at the end of this history metaphysics would no longer be capable of keeping watch over being by itself. A conclusion follows: "the Christian is called to be the guardian of metaphysics in our time."[29] The author is not responding to nihilism, which is absent from the text, but a combination of the misfortunes of the times and the forgetting of being. However, do not these misfortunes and this forgetting find their accomplished form (in both a historical and conceptual sense) in nihilism? Nihilism makes it so that nothing is worth anything (any longer). Henceforth, everything is the same. And if Nietzsche relegates God to the world beyond, which is itself only a dream bereft of all reality, then the time of the last man has come, that of the superman has not yet come, and between the two is the time when the "meaning of being," an expression which is not Nietzsche's, is hidden in the will to power which is not yet truly at work. Nietzsche despairs of metaphysics even if Heidegger sees in him the last metaphysician. He does not pose the question of being, even if Heidegger says that the will to power is nothing less than the being of beings. And if, in conjunction with Balthasar, we admit that Heidegger himself thinks within the time of nihilism and does not provide us with the means to overcome it (which cannot be admitted without nuance, since Heidegger truly makes ours the duty of "thinking"), then theology can claim to exercise a vicarial function. Not only is it occupied with the splendor of God, but it also watches over the splendor of creation, and this double task allows it to watch over being and its "meaning."

The God of Schelling is the "Lord of being." Man appears in Heidegger as the "Shepherd of being."[30] In Balthasar, finally, the Christian becomes the guardian of being. But between Heidegger and Balthasar one difference among others ought not to pass by unseen: the Christian's mission is a substitute. (Almost) everything is set up so that *Herrlichkeit* III/2 can suggest the necessity of this substitution: the history that the theologian recounts for us is the history of what we have lost, whether it be the heritage of the Greeks or the Germans, passing by Ruysbroeck and many others. We just mentioned a kind of mysticism (which we have called spiritual), and this forces us to admit that the "domain" of metaphysics, such as Balthasar envisaged it, is vaster than the historians of philosophy are accustomed to say. The precise words of the author remind us that the "mission" to accomplish in these dark times is not entrusted to the theologian (or to Christian philosophers, whatever we understand that term to mean) but, more simply, to Christians: "christlicher Auftrag." As Balthasar maps it out, the domain of metaphysics is peopled with poets and spiritual authors as much as with theologians and philosophers. The task of providing a "comprehensive and contemporary metaphysics" is assigned to Christians as Christians.[31] And if this is the case, then we find ourselves turning again to the article entitled "Theology and Sanctity." Who will provide such a metaphysics and how will they do it? And, in a complementary way, who will incarnate it (live it) and how will they do it? Balthasar's closing lines leave no doubt about the necessity of a theoretical work (nor about the fact that this work has already begun in his writings). However, this work is only thinkable as stemming from a *theōria:* Balthasar did not hesitate to say that the only adequate Christian response posed to Nietzsche was by Thérèse of Lisieux. With the notion of "Christian mission" we are necessarily sent back to a theology that is lived before it is made doctrine, a theology that can be thought only if it is incarnated in a *vita philosophica vel theologica.* Since we are dealing with the saint, does he, finally, do the work of thinking? Words are hardly even necessary to observe that Heideggerian *Gedanc,* formulated, of course, outside (almost) any religious horizon, is not too far removed from a (secularized . . .) *opus Dei* lived as perpetual doxology. The saint's ambition is to pray, not to think (but he can receive the mission to think, to become a professor, etc.). It is probably not useful at all (supposing that we can call Joe Blow a saint, which is never self-evident, since sanctity is perfectly capable of passing incognito) to say that the work of prayer is akin to the work of thought, or even that they are two faces of the same work. Being unable ourselves to describe adequately the experience of the saint, we can describe that of the theologian. We will simply suppose that the theologian wants to live in the school of the saints, though of course he is in their school all the while pursuing a conceptual work. And here finally, it is possible to ask whether his work of thinking accomplishes an exclusively Christian mission or whether it participates in this mission with philosophy.

We finally come to our title, which speaks, therefore, of theological *thinking*. Is it self-evident that theology thinks? Or would it not be necessary to say, rather, that it can and ought to think? And on the other hand, is it not obvious that there is no lack of theological disciplines duly recognized in which the work of thinking does not seem to have a place (the best example being Church history)? We will respond in several steps. (a) To say that theology is capable of thinking is no different from what Balthasar told us. Theology is guardian of all the meanings that nihilism abolishes (but still, it would be necessary for theology to be aware of this . . .). Theology carries out its work today in the time of the devastation of the universe of values. And with God eminently taking part in what nihilism annuls, theology certainly does not itself resurrect God, but bears the mission of giving meaning to "God." This is a new phenomenon. It is new because nihilism (and Nietzsche) are not attacking God in general but the Christian God—the God that theology or a philosophy of revelation speaks about. In its classical form atheism is an anti-theism and as such it attacks any such entity that merits more or less the name of God. In its Nietzschean and nihilist form (if we are allowed to say that Nietzsche is a nihilist at all . . .) it attacks the God of history (refuted by the theory of the eternal return of the same), the Father of Jesus Christ and the crucified God. The theologian must recognize that the opposition Dionysus against the Crucified is not rhetorical. The *logos* that the theologian claims to follow is the *logos* of the cross. This *logos* can be refused in the name of other rationalities. It can be refused in the name of the absence of any candidate for the title of God, if the dead God "remains dead." For some time now theology has spoken of God in the face of an anti-theist atheism. Its first task would therefore be to elaborate the first discourse that it will have ever held, facing a critique not aimed at any God whatsoever but at the Christian God and him alone. (b) Every new situation calls for new tasks. Theology can fruitfully repeat itself. Like the philosophical concept of progress, its concept is complex, and includes the permanent rereading of its sources, and often a return to these sources. Now it is certainly a fruitless return to the sources that we generally see when we encounter those returns decorated with the prefix "neo," Neo-Thomism, Neo-Patristics, Neo-Palamism. And in order to avoid a sterile return to the sources, the work of thought will necessarily be the double work of rereading and rewriting. Rewriting is not copying. On the contrary, rewriting is more simply the production of a new text within new horizons—emphatically not a text that breaks with the first text, but a text that responds to questions to which the first text did not respond for the very good reason that it did not know them. If theology wants to think, its primary interest will not be in wanting to make progress but in backtracking. Theology will probably find in its past, and not in an imagined future, the necessary resources to go further than nihilism. (We should add here that it will find in an elementary fidelity to its own ways of reasoning the means to refuse the eternal return of the same and to say that God is dead but does not remain dead: in this case, an indispensable repetition requires no backtracking.) (c) A theology is perfectly possible that we would have to say does not think even though it carries out its work with all probity. A theology that is withdrawn into what it gives to be believed—for example, under the form of a positivism of revelation or a strict respect for the "revealed given"—can do many things: it can announce, narrate, write a critical history of its sources, etc., but now and then one has to acknowledge that it leaves its object unthought. The theologian can do the work of thinking, but he can also leave unthought the content of his discourse. What does this mean? First it means that the faithful repetition of a kerygma or credo is probably a condition sine qua non, but this necessity does not make for a sufficient condition. The continuity of the kerygma in the discontinuity of times requires rereading and rewriting.

To specify further, we link together thinking and tradition. The art of thinking is theologically traditional. If there should be a theological thinking in addition to a theological discourse, then it does not come about out of a rupture. It arises, and this is something totally different, in a perpetual movement of transmission that we should understand as a perpetual process of deepening, sometimes involving backtracking. When we say tradition we do not mean that this or that—a text, above all, or a practice—is preserved and transmitted from an origin, and that there is nothing else to do but to preserve and transmit it ourselves. On the contrary, tradition involves the complex language of life. The last (Catholic) debate on tradition to excite a lively and legitimate interest is the one between Lennerz and Geiselmann, which saw the success of Geiselmann's position and its sanctioning by the theology of the Second Vatican Council.[32] Geiselmann represented the now extinct Tübingen School: the concept of "living tradition" is purely a product of this school. Bringing together thinking, life, and tradition would certainly allow us to behold theology as such. Thinking has to be living and life has to deal with death: there are after all dead thoughts, which were living but for us are only vestiges. About the theology that we desire to think today, let us not delude ourselves: it will perhaps think only within the conditions that characterize today and will be revivified tomorrow only by being reread and rewritten. (Though all theology does not deserve to be reread and rewritten!) Theologies (and, of course, philosophies) that do not think abound. They are lost in mechanical repetition.

FROM THEOLOGY TO THEOLOGICAL THINKING

The existence of dead theology, which no one can bring back to life, motivates us in any case to choose living theologies, set within a tradition that is not an unadulterated, objective transmission from hand to hand, that is, a tradition that performs the work of thinking.

We have implicitly recognized a break that we should name more precisely. Theology lives within the element of tradition, whereas philosophy knows only those micro-traditions of schools and movements. (Theology knows them as well but integrates them into a vaster history.) To be sure, philosophy is also a matter of rereading and rewriting, except that it grants these a scientific status and reads its history with the help of a scientific concept of progress. Thinking within tradition and thinking without recourse to an encompassing concept of tradition are in any case both a matter of thinking. And if we recall our definitively acquired incapacity to trace any limit between philosophy and theology, we will be able to go a little further and declare ourselves incapable of strictly demarcating philosophical thinking and theological thinking. There are some clear cases of delimitation: the philosophy of mathematics is only philosophical; the theory of the ministry of the anointing of the sick is only theological. Yet theology thinks about God before being interested in the ministry of the anointing of the sick (and when it is interested in the ministry of the anointing of the sick, it does it without thinking, rendering witness to a *traditum* and without entailing a living tradition). And if it thinks about God or Christ or the Church or the Eucharist, it ought to agree that philosophy thinks about them too. It is also often appropriate—this has been our central proposal—to make the labels disappear in order to be content with letting thinking happen wherever one thinks. Will a philosophical Christology allow us to overcome nihilism or is this the task of a theological Christology? The question is absurd, for all that matters is what we are thinking and the fact that we are thinking. On the one hand, we are called to think *about God*. On the other hand, we are called to *think* about God. The task that is assigned to us, to overcome nihilism, is a task that is neither properly philosophical nor theological. It ought to be sufficient for us that it is a task for thinking. Thinking is plural: a good proof of this is that it can have either a traditional or a nontraditional character. However, this plurality can be lived in a unity of questions and a convergence of answers. We can therefore lose all interest in knowing which discipline we are practicing when we take an interest in God and in the things of God: we will simply be judged by the power of what we say. Power and the will to power, after all, are, after Nietzsche, what permit the overcoming of nihilism. In its own manner, thinking must will to be powerful—unless it is, more simply, essential to its being. This slightly surprising mode of the will to power, first lived in "thanks," is the standard by which thinking will be judged—or rather, that by which one will judge that it truly was a work of thought.

Notes

1. A detailed account of Lacoste's intellectual itinerary can be found in J. Schrijvers, *An Introduction to Jean-Yves Lacoste* (Farnham, UK: Ashgate, 2012), 1–14.

2. J.-Y. Lacoste, *Note sur le temps* (Paris: PUF, 1994), 41, characterizing steps taken by Heidegger in *Sein und Zeit* beginning at §43.

3. In short, there is no theological turn in the phenomenology of Jean-Yves Lacoste. This did not escape the notice of the most determined critic of that "turn," Dominique Janicaud; see his *Phenomenology and the "Theological Turn"* (New York: Fordham University Press, 2000), 100n23.

4. J.-Y. Lacoste, "Histoire," in *Dictionnaire critique de théologie* (Paris: PUF, 1998), 543. Chris Hackett makes the same point with reference to this encyclopedia article in an interview with Lacoste to appear in C. Hackett and T. Dika, "The Quiet Power of the Possible: Interviews in Contemporary French Phenomenology" (New York: Fordham University Press, forthcoming). I wish to thank Hackett for sharing this interview with me as I completed this introduction.

5. See especially J.-Y. Lacoste, *Expérience et Absolu* (Paris: PUF, 1994), §29, pp. 92–93; translated by Mark Raftery-Skehan as *Experience and the Absolute: Disputed Questions on the Humanity of Man* (New York: Fordham University Press, 2004), 75–76.

6. J. Ladrière, *La foi chrétienne et le Destin de la raison* (Paris: Cerf, 2006), 57–76.

7. This is meant to remain clear of any philosophy or theology of man. Lacoste appears to accept Heidegger's claim that the latter are ontical and therefore derived conceptions (see *Sein und Zeit* §10), yet without submitting their entire question to the premises of Heidegger's ontologi-

cal project (on this, see esp. *Expérience et Absolu*, 27, 209 [*Experience and the Absolute*, 22, 173–74]). It is worth noting that the subtitle of *Expérience et Absolu* is *Questions disputées sur l'humanité de l'homme.*

8. *Expérience et Absolu*, 41n1 (*Experience and the Absolute*, 200–201n9). As I am about to note, this is the site of a dispute with Rahner's transcendental theological anthropology. But the polemic should not be disjoined from a stake that is strictly phenomenological: "The world is not the field of theophany, it is that of the chiaroscuro" (44 [36]).

9. See J.-Y. Lacoste, "Le désir et l'inexigible: Pour lire H. de Lubac," in *Le monde et l'absence d'oeuvre* (Paris: PUF, 2000), 23–54; and "Dieu connaissable comme aimable: Par-delà 'foi et raison,'" in *Phénomenalité de Dieu: Neuf études* (Paris: Cerf, 2008), esp. 88–90, translated by J. Bloechl as "On Knowing God through Loving Him: Beyond 'Faith and Reason,'" in *Christianity and Secular Reason: Classical Themes and Modern Problems*, ed. Bloechl (Notre Dame: University of Notre Dame Press, 2012), esp. 128–30.

10. *Expérience et Absolu*, 231–33 (*Experience and the Absolute*, 193–94).

11. S. Breton, *The Word and the Cross* (New York: Fordham University Press, 2002), 31–32.

12. *Expérience et Absolu*, 216–17 (*Experience and the Absolute*, 180–82).

13. Perhaps this signals no more than a predilection. One finds it again in the fact that Lacoste's contributions to the collaborative volume *Histoire de la théologie* (Paris: Seuil, 2009) concentrate on the sixteenth through eighteenth centuries and the nineteenth through twentieth centuries (285–364, 367–470). In any case, his many other publications make it quite clear that this is certainly not a matter of limited competence with other periods.

14. *Dictionnaire critique de théologie*, 523.

15. In D. Janicaud, *Heidegger en France*, vol. 2: *Entretiens* (Paris: Albin Michel, 2001), 191–92.

16. Even before the nine essays collected in *Phénomenalité de Dieu* (2008), several in *Le monde et l'absence d'oeuvre* (Paris: PUF, 2000) and *Présence et parousie* (Geneva: Ad solem, 2006) pursue this same project, though others in that latter text also begin to explore some of the concerns taken up in the Richard Lectures published in this volume.

17. J.-Y. Lacoste, *Être et danger* (Paris: Cerf, 2011).

18. For this way of reading John of the Cross in a manner that anticipates the position taken here by Lacoste, see M. Huot de Longchamp, *Lectures de Jean de la Croix: Essai d'anthropologie mystique* (Paris: Beauchesne, 1981).

ONE. Theōria, vita philosophica, *and Christian Experience*

1. On the history of the concept of philosophy in antiquity, see the report of A.-M. Malingrey, *"Philosophia": Étude d'un groupe de mots dans la littérature grecque, des présocratiques au IVe siècle après J.-C.* (Paris: Klincksiek, 1961).

2. See, for example, *Krisis*, *Husserliana* 6, 15.

3. In Martin Heidegger, *Platons, Sophistes, Gesamtausgabe* (hereafter *GA*) 19 (Frankfurt am Main: Klostermann, 1992).

4. Thus, with a good deal of anachronism but also some truth, the Aristotelian theory of causality can be treated as foundation for a "science of being." See M. Bastit, *Les quatre causes de l'être selon la philosophie première d'Aristote* (Louvain-la-Neuve: Peeters, 2002).

5. Heidegger, *Platons, Sophistes*, §§9–26.

6. Thus Aristotle. See Rémi Brague, *Aristote et la question du monde: Essai sur le contexte cosmologique et anthropologique de l'ontologie* (Paris: PUF, 1988).

7. See the synthesis of Martin Hengel, *Judaismus und Hellenismus*, translated by John Bowden as *Judaism and Hellenism: Studies in Their Encounter in Palestine in the Early Hellenistic Period* (London: SCM Press, 1974).

8. Anna Miura-Stange, *Celsus und Origenes: Das gemeinsame ihrer Weltanschauung nach den acht Büchern des Origenes gegen Celsus* (Giessen: A. Töpelmann, 1926).

9. Jürgen Habermas, "Vorpolitische Grundlagen demokratischen Rechtstaates?," in Habermas and Joseph Ratzinger, *Dialektik der Sakularisierung* (Freiburg: Herder, 2005), 15–37.

10. [This phrase is in English in the original. —Trans.]

11. Clement of Alexandria, *Stromata* 6.8, 67.

12. The examination of their teachings supports the hypothesis. See Henri Crouzel, *Origen et Plotin: Comparaisons doctrinales* (Paris: Téqui, 1992).

13. See Yochanan Lewy, *Chaldean Oracles and Theurgy: Mysticism, Magic and Platonism in the Later Roman Empire*, new ed., by Marcel Tardieu (Paris: Études augustinennes, 1978).

14. See Guy G. Stroumsa, *La fin du sacrifice: Les mutations religieuses de l'Antiquité tardive* (Paris: Odile Jacob, 2005).

15. See, of course, Peter Brown, "The Rise and Function of Holy Men in Late Antiquity," in *Society and the Holy in Late Antiquity* (Berkeley: University of California Press, 1982). [The phrase "holy men" is in English in the original. —Trans.]

16. Hans Urs von Balthasar, "Philosophie, Christentum, Mönchtum," in *Sponsa Verbi*, Skizzen zur Theologie 2 (Einsiedeln: Johannes Verlag, 1961), 349–87.

17. See Derwas J. Chitty, *The Desert a City: An Introduction to the Study of Egyptian and Palestinian Monasticism under the Christian Empire* (Oxford: Blackwell, 1966).

18. On this subject see Donald MacKinnon, "Tillich, Frege, Kittel: Some Reflections on a Dark Theme," in *Explorations in Theology*, vol. 5 (London: SCM Press, 1979), 129–37.

19. Hans Urs von Balthasar, "Theologie und Heiligkeit," in *Verbum Caro*, Skizzen zur Theologie 1 (Einsiedeln: Johannes Verlag, 1960), 195–225.

TWO. *Philosophy, Theology, and the Academy*

1. See Henri Crouzel, *Origène et la philosophie* (Paris: Aubier, 1962), 103–37.

2. *Stoicorum Veterum Fragmenta*, ed. J. von Arnim, 3 vols. (Leipzig, 1903–5), 1:537.

3. See, for example, Alvin Plantinga, *God, Freedom, and Evil* (Grand Rapids: Eerdmans, 1974), 85–112.

4. See Henry Donneaud, *Théologie et intelligence de la foi au XIIIe siècle* (Paris: Parole et Silence, 2006).

5. On this subject, see, of course, Marie-Dominique Chenu, *La théologie comme science au XIIIe siècle*, 3rd ed. (Paris: Librairie Philosophique J. Vrin, 1957).

6. Proposition 212 in the catalog of theses condemned in Paris. See Roland Hissette, *Enquête sur les 219 articles condamnés à Paris le 7 mars 1277* (Louvain: Librairie Philosophique J. Vrin, 1977), 300–304. Following Hissette we observe that there is truly a place for humility in Siger of Brabant, the author targeted by the condemnation, but that humility is "the virtue for little people," whereas magnanimity is the virtue of the "perfect."

7. See Olivier-Thomas Venard, *Thomas d'Aquin, poète théologien*, 3 vols. (Geneva: Ad Solem, 2003–9).

8. The most charming formulations are certainly those of M. Th.-L. Penido, *Le rôle de l'analogie en théologie dogmatique* (Paris: J. Vrin, 1931), 223–24.

9. See his brief to the Grand Inquisitor of Spain, where, in taking up the non-conclusion of the congregations *de auxiliis*, he affirms outright that the Church encourages the plurality of theological schools (DS 2564–65).

10. Times change: see (even the title of) Richard Schaeffler, *Philosophische Einübung in die Theologie*, 3 vols. (Fribourg: Verlag Karl Alber, 2004–8).

11. See Husserl, *Krisis*, §9h.

12. The concept of non-philosophy appears in C. A. Eschenmeyer's *Die Philosophie in ihrem Übergang zur Nichtphilosophie* (Erlangen, 1803) in order to designate the religious domain by contrast to the theological. It does not lack relevance to our purpose.

13. [This word appears in English in the original. —Trans.]

14. [This word appears in English in the original. In British politics it signifies more or less the equivalent of an "independent" in American politics or *non-inscrit* in France. —Trans.]

THREE. *Philosophy, Theology, and the Task of Thinking*

1. It is a known fact that there have been illegitimately scientific claims (see the *Wissenschaftslehre* of Fichte or the *Phenomenology of Spirit*) or exorbitant claims to be scientific (Husserl). But German Idealism understood by science what we would call rigorous knowledge. And in Husserl it is less a foundation for a science that counts itself among the other sciences than a project for an archscience that totally overflows the limits of Galilean science.

2. See Thomas F. Torrance, *Theological Science* (London: Oxford University Press, 1969).

3. An analogous effort was made after Torrance to show the existence of parallel methods in philosophy and theology, in Husserl and Barth. See H. J. Adriaanse, *Zu den Sachen selbst: Versuch einer Konfrontation der Theologie Karl Barths mit der phänomenologischen Philosophie Edmund Husserls* (The Hague: Mouton, 1974).

4. See Martin Heidegger, *Phänomenologie und Theologie*, in *Wegmarken*, GA 9, 45–78.

5. See John Hick, "Theology and Verification," *Theology Today* 17 (April 1960): 12–31.

6. See the extreme position of Wolfhart Pannenberg, for whom divine revelation is given to whoever has eyes to see: *Offenbarung als Geschichte* (Göttingen: Vandenhoek and Ruprecht, 1961), 98, thesis 3.

7. Thus in Alfred Schütz, *Der sinnliche Aufbau der sozialen Welt* (Vienna: J. Springer, 1932).

8. See above, n. 3.

9. Rudolph Bultmann and Martin Heidegger, *Briefwechsel 1925–1975* (Frankfurt am Main: Klostermann; Tübingen: Mohr Siebeck, 2009), letter of December 18, 1928.

10. Jörg Splett, *Die Trinitätslehre G. W. F. Hegels* (Fribourg-Munich: Verlag Karl Alber, 1984).

11. See Xavier Tilliette, *Le Christ des philosophes: Du Maître de sagesse au divin témoin* (Namur: Culture et Verité, 1993), and *Le Christ de la philosophie: Prolégomènes à une christologie philosophique* (Paris: Editions du Cerf, 1990).

12. See Jacques Colette, *Kierkegaard et la non-philosophie* (Paris: Gallimard, 1994); see above, chap. 2, n. 12.

13. Heidegger, *Sein und Zeit,* §45, n. 6.

14. Edith Stein, *Science of the Cross: A Study of St. John of the Cross* (London: Burns & Oates, 1960).

15. Heidegger, *Was heißt Denken?, GA* 8, 9.

16. Ibid., 6, 7, et passim.

17. See Vincent Carraud (*Pascal et la philosophie* [Paris: PUF, 1992]), to whom we owe the invaluable concept of a "non-chronological exit from metaphysics."

18. See Heidegger, *Über den Anfang, GA* 70.

19. See the lecture course of 1926–27, *Geschichte der Philosophie von Thomas von Aquin bis Kant, GA* 23, given as soon as he finished composing *Sein und Zeit,* which prolonged indefinitely the book that will remain incomplete.

20. Franz Rosenzweig, "The New Thinking," in *Philosophical and Theological Writings,* trans. and ed. Paul W. Franks and Michael L. Morgan (Indianapolis: Hackett, 2000), 109–39.

21. Franz Rosenzweig, *Hegel und der Staat* (Munich: R. Oldenbourg, 1920).

22. See Rudolph Bultmann, "Welchen Sinn has es, von Gott zu reden?," in *Glauben und Verstehen,* vol. 1 (Tübingen: Mohr, 1933), 26–37.

23. Two examples: the dialogue between theology and science already mentioned, undertaken in the wake of T. F. Torrance, and the appearance of a new discipline, "theology and literature," which we owe to Jean-Pierre Jossua.

24. See F. C. Bauer, *Christliche Gnosis, oder die christliche Religionsphilosophie in ihrer geschichtlichen Entwicklung* (Tübingen: C. F. Osiander, 1935).

25. See F. A. Staudenmaier, *Darstellung und Kritik des hegelschen Systems—aus dem Standpunkt der christlichen Philosophie* (Mayence, 1844). A theology is hidden behind the mask of "Christian philosophy."

26. The expression is from Leszek Kolakowski, *Chrétiens sans église: La conscience religieuse et le lien confessionnel au 17e siècle,* trans. Anna Posner (Paris: Gallimard, 1969).

27. See the *Instruction on the Ecclesial Vocation of the Theologian*, published in Rome, May 24, 1990.

28. Balthasar, *Herrlichkeit* III/2, *Im Raum der Metaphysik* (Einsiedeln: Johannes Verlag, 1965), 2 vols., continual pagination.

29. Ibid., 983 [Lacoste translates the German into French, but I reproduce the quotation as it appears in the translation by Oliver Davies et al., *The Glory of the Lord*, vol. 5: *The Realm of Metaphysics in the Modern Age* (Edinburgh: T. and T. Clark; San Francisco: Ignatius Press, 1991), 656. —Trans.].

30. Heidegger, "Brief über den Humanismus," *Wegmarken*, GA 9, 331.

31. Balthasar, *Herrlichkeit* III/2, 980 [*Glory of the Lord*, 652. —Trans.].

32. See Josef Rupert Geiselmann, *Die heilige Schrift und die Tradition* (Fribourg im Breisgau: Herder, 1962).

Index

Abelard, Peter, 38, 39, 40, 48; *Sentences*, 46, 49–50, 61
academy, the. *See* schools; universities
Academy, the (Athens), 16
Adriaanse, H. J., 68
Alexander, 12
Alexandrian School, 35, 41
angelic life, 23
Anselm of Bec: integrated philosophy and theology of, 41, 43; "kneeling" theology of, 80; *Monologion*, 42; "proof" by, 81; and school at Bec, 36
Antiochian School, 20, 35
antiphilosophism, 12, 38
Aquinas. *See* Thomas Aquinas
Aristotelianism: and Scholasticism, 51; substance and accidents, 69–70; and theology as a speciality, 44, 46
Aristotle: commentaries on works by, 45, 55; and Hegel, 59; logic of, 5; moral philosophy of, 5–6; scientific theories of, 5; and theory, 4; theory of causality of, 45–46, 93n4; translation of works by, 31, 41; and the West, 18
arts: faculty of, 53; liberal, 42; technical, 42, 43
ascesis, 21, 25

Athanasius, 20
atheism, 14, 86
Augustine of Hippo: and "Christian philosophy," 19, 31; *Confessions*, 32–33; "kneeling" theology of, 80; and "Platonic books," 17, 38; rule of, 33; and theory of time, 43
Aurelius, Marcus, 11
Averroism, 69

Bacon, Francis: and the Enlightenment, 57; epistemology of, 54, 56; and theology, 55; and traits of science, 65
Balthasar, Hans Urs von: *Herrlichkeit* III/2, 84, 85; and "kneeling" theology, 24, 80; and metaphysics, 85; on monastic life, 21, 22; originality of, 69; on sanctity, 24; "Theology and Sanctity," 85; and theology and thinking, 86
barbarism, 13
Barth, Karl: on Anselm, 41; character of, 23; *Dogmatics*, 59, 60; originality of, 69
being, 7–8, 12, 84; and philosophy, 1, 2; and transcendence, 8. *See also* metaphysics
Bellarmine, Robert, and Galileo Galilei, 39
Benedict, Saint, rule of, 40–41

Benedict XIV, Pope, 51
Bernard of Clairvaux, 38, 40, 50
Bernini, 26
Bérulle, Pierre de, 57
Bible, the. *See* scriptures (Christian)
Biel, Gabriel, 55
bios philosophikos, 22. *See also*
    "philosophical life," the
bios theōretikos, 5, 22. *See also*
    "theoretical life," the
Boethius, 34, 38; *Consolation of*
    Philosophy, 31–32
Boethius of Dacia, 48, 52
Bonaventure, 51, 55, 61; and
    Aristotelianism, 46
Bossuet, Jacques-Bénigne, 60
Bucer, Martin, 56
Bultmann, Rudolph, 18

Calvin, John, 56
Cantor, Georg, 25, 71
Carmelites, 22, 54–55
Catholic Church hierarchy, 70, 82
Celsus, 12, 14; *True Discourse*, 16
Chaldean Oracles, 18, 19
charism and grace, 24
Chartres, 35, 38
Christian exclusivism, 15
Christian experience, 63, 64; and
    philosophical life, 31, 32, 48;
    —, as distinct from each other,
    12–17; —, as equivalent, 17–27;
    and *theōria*, 20–29
Christianity: and ethics, 20–21;
    and knowledge, 13–14; as non-
    philosophy, 13, 17; and paganism,
    14–16, 20; and philosophy, 13,
    17, 18, 43; positivity of, 63;
    and reason, 15, 16–17, 18; and
    wisdom, 14
Christian philosophy, 18, 19, 20, 21
Christian praxis, 21
Cistercians, 36. *See also* monasticism
Cleanthes: hymn to Zeus, 33, 34
Clement of Alexandria, 17, 19
Concept of Anxiety, The (Kierke-
    gaard), 72

condemnations, ecclesiastical,
    46–47, 48
Confession of Augsburg, 58
Confessions (Augustine of Hippo),
    32–33
conflict of philosophy and theology
    faculties, 70. *See* theology and
    philosophy
connaissance, 66. *See also* knowledge
consideratio. See *theōria*
Consolation of Philosophy (Boethius),
    31, 32
contemplation, 2, 8, 21, 25, 40; and
    science, 4. See also *theōria*
conversio morum, 23
Corpus Leontianum, 50
cosmogony, 5
cosmos, 4, 5, 14, 15; and the world, 7
Crisis (Husserl), 4, 67
cross, the: and the rational, 12
Cynics, the, 21, 22; and philo-
    sophical life, 3; and *theōria*, 3
Cyril of Alexandria, 23, 61

De primo principio (Duns Scotus), 52
Descartes, René, 54, 66
desert fathers, 28. *See also*
    monasticism, in Egypt
Diadochus of Photice, 28
dialectic, 38, 40, 42
Diderot, Denis, and Jean le Rond
    d'Alembert: *Encyclopedia*, 57
Dionysus, 87
disciplines, particularity of, 69
Disputatio contra theologiam
    scholasticism (Luther), 55
divine, the, 15, 16
Dogmatics (Barth), 59, 60
doxology: and *Gedanc*, 85; and
    instruction, 28, 42

Eckhart, Meister, 55, 61
Elements (Proclus), 18
Encyclopedia (Diderot and
    d'Alembert), 57
"enframing." See *Gestell*
Enlightenment, 14, 56, 57, 58, 63

scientificity, 66, 67, 72, 74; and
utility, 76
Scotus, John Duns: *De primo
principio*, 52
Scotus Erigena, John, 37, 38, 53
scriptures (Christian): interpretation
of, 19, 20, 55; philosophical
competency of, 12; and the
Sentences, 49
Second Vatican Council, 88
secularization, 14, 16
Sentences (Abelard), 46, 49–50, 61
Siger of Brabant, 48, 52
Sixth Cartesian Meditation (Fink), 8
Socrates: as philosopher, 3, 4, 34;
and the real, 2; and *theōria*, 3, 4
sophia: and knowledge, 4; and
wisdom, 4, 5
Sophists, the, 3
spiritual literature, 73–74; and
science, 74–75
Star of Redemption, The (Rosenzweig),
79
Staudenmaier, F. A., 82
Stein, Edith, 22, 25, 74
Stoicism, 11, 17–18, 20
Saint Victor, masters of, 36
Summa contra gentiles (Thomas
Aquinas), 52
Summa theologiae (Thomas Aquinas), 52
supernaturalism, 13, 57

teaching, 49, 50
technology: and nihilism, 79, 83;
reign of, 4, 77; and science, 76
technology and science, 4
Tempier, Étienne, 48
Teresa of Avila, Saint, 73
Teresa of Avila (sculpture by Bernini),
25
Tertullian, 12, 13
thanking and thinking, 77, 90
Theodoret, 13; *Therapy*, 38
theologia irregenitorum, 24
theologian, definition of, 24
theological experience, 42. *See also*
Christian experience

theological life, the, 25, 29, 86;
integral with philosophical
life, 31–42; separate from
philosophical life, 43–59;
and theological work, 40;
and theology, 37. *See also*
monasticism; theology and
philosophy
theological work, 29, 40, 80. *See also*
prayer
theology: ascetic, 73, 74; autonomy
of, 44; breadth of, 82, 84; Catholic, 56–57; discrediting of, 65;
disintegration of, 61; and *Gedanc*,
80; "kneeling," 24, 26, 28, 80;
and knowledge, 38, 39, 40; —,
and the sciences, 63–66, 68,
72–73; "lived theology," 22, 24;
living or dead, 88–89; Lutheran,
56, 57; medieval, 52; monastic,
48, 49; mystical, 73, 74; narrative,
33; nominalist, 55; as non-
philosophy, 62; and philosophy
(*see* theology and philosophy);
and prayer, 32, 33, 40, 41, 42;
pre-Scholastic, 50; Protestant, 56;
as "pure science," 55; "queen of
sciences," 54; scholastic, 46; and
science, 72, 73–75; as science,
48, 57, 58, 62, 64, 66; as *scientia*,
48, 54, 63, 65; sources of, 87;
spiritual, 60, 73, 74; and theological life, 37; and *theōria*, 37, 40,
85; and thinking, 80–90, 87; and
tradition, 89; and universities, 50,
51, 56, 57, 64, 94n9
theology and philosophy, 1, 13, 27;
abolition of boundaries between,
82–83; as one discipline, 31–42;
—, with theology dominant,
34–42; shared frontier of, 68–73;
as two specialities, 43–62, 68–69;
—, in mutual conflict, 52–59; —,
subsequent to mutual conflict,
59–62, 81
"Theology and Sanctity" (Balthasar),
85